Carol Adyeeri Adams

Grit of Love

A memoir

Editors: Chris Ategeka and Lindsey Hampton
Cover Design: Adam Renvoize
Interior Design: Jennifer Stimson

Printed in the United States of America by Positude Publishing

Library of Congress Control Number: 2023900390

ISBN: 979-8-9876032-0-8

POSITUDE
PUBLISHING

Table of Contents

Introduction

I am living in Uganda!!! I sometimes wake up amazed to be in Fort Portal, running an NGO and a hostel. I am quite an unlikely person for this work. Many situations are sad and frustrating. The paperwork is tedious, and daily decisions are exhausting. One experiences loneliness. Health care is poor and a bit scary. Despite the negative aspects, I cherish my country Uganda and the people and the work. I relish the beautiful mountains and green pastures filled with cows, the many beautiful birds and flowers and warm weather. I do not miss television and the rush of life in the US. I am home here.

God does not always choose the most qualified, bold, and strong person. Whatever is being accomplished in this small part of the world is all through God's support and wisdom. My belief influences my choices and my work. All major decisions have been directed by God. When faced with daunting alternatives, I need and make time for prayer and quiet time.

Why have I written this book? That question has chased me for an answer for some time. As I look back on 75 years, there has been a major theme – God's love and faithfulness from the start. God is behind all things in our life. However, it wasn't until I freed myself from society's unrealistic expectations and embraced my own superpowers that I could authentically stand in God's grace and do the work I was called to do. Anyway, this book is not about any theological set of beliefs nor filled with Bible verses (though you will find a few) to prove my thinking. I am not here to evangelize. Rather, I share a miraculous journey where God never gave up on me. I have travelled through Europe and throughout the US, including living on Maui, Hawaii. I have met wonderful, dedicated and loving Christians all along the way.

Yet, I dislike religion as it separates more than unites. Many church leaders are arrogant with rules and dogma that lack compassion. I have travelled to Catholic, Anglican, Pentecostal and other churches in my fundraising trips. It is so frustrating how each group believes that they are 100% correct and any other beliefs are wrong. Somewhere along the lines, compassion has been lost. I will not even begin to argue concerning my personal beliefs. I have become independent in my thinking. I no longer let people of the church influence me in any negative way. I cannot think of God as ready to strike anyone down because they do not jump through religious hoops.

In the last 24 years living in Uganda, I have been taught so much by the very people I came to help. The poverty is huge. Challenges of sickness and wars and hunger are overwhelming, but the courage and faith of many is truly inspiring. The culture is different and often hard to understand. However, different is not necessarily bad. I get quite upset with visitors from developed countries who feel they must teach their thinking and seem to look towards the Ugandan people as if they are ignorant and beneath them. I have met many sincere, devout missionaries but have also met those who make me cringe and even hesitate to call myself a missionary. I have made many mistakes through my years here, and I thank the Ugandans for being accepting, patient, and loving.

I think the most important thing in life can be summed up in one word – LOVE—love of humanity no matter what, and love of God. No one person needs to come to Africa or do any spectacular service. With more love and less judgement, the world could change. I am saddened by homeless people, elderly forgotten in long term care homes, immigrants, people with special needs, and perhaps just family and neighbors who go overlooked. All of us have the ability to make a positive impact in the world. This is just my story.

I do not want to come across as some sort of a saint or suffering missionary. I am neither, and I certainly am not saving Uganda or even Western Uganda. I am simply trying to help give people hope and young people a path to a brighter future through self-sufficiency. I get annoyed with "missionaries" who whine about all they have "sacrificed" in order to help the "poor" Africans. If they don't like it here – GO HOME. They play the part of the martyr on Facebook yet live better here than they could in their native countries with servants, fancy houses and cars, flying home yearly. I find it strange that when people come to a developing country through most mission agencies, they are required to raise huge amounts of money. A fair amount ends up paying salaries for the agency and luxurious living conditions.

When I felt my calling to Africa, I did not want to ask for money for myself. I came without agency backing and am so glad I did it my own way. Had I come with an agency, I wouldn't have had the choice to stay here during the ADF war. Perhaps that would have been wiser and safer, but I feel that having lived in the village and similarly to the Ugandan people, I was and am accepted. I think I was the only *mzungu* (foreigner) they had ever seen in the queue for water, and I was a bit embarrassed that people would help me carry the jerry cans to my car. I feel so fortunate to have been closer to the lives of the people even though I live much more comfortably than most. I don't think the missionaries living in expensive rentals will ever have the wonderful feeling of being a real part of the country.

For you to understand this book, I need to explain a few things.

When I first came here, I was so overwhelmed that I talked on a cassette tape to process my experiences and feelings. To complete this book, I purchased a cassette player. I can now listen again to my original thoughts. I have been here so long that what used to amaze me is now common.

I guess living through the ADF war and some of the

other crazy things I have faced is not exactly every day normal. Strange as it sounds, it almost feels normal now. When I first arrived, there were times I was quite scared. You just keep on going. I learned that there is always a way, and just to hang in there. In the early days when I travel outside of Uganda, the first thing I wanted was a looooong hot shower and a pizza. Now, we even have pizza in Fort Portal.

To protect real people and even myself, I occasionally omit or mask the names of powerful, yet corrupt, individuals. Because some names are quite common – Sam, for example – I might introduce someone by a full name and then use some nickname, abbreviation, or middle name. Other times, I'll use their more Western name because the person's given name is unfamiliar and I'm trying to be clear who is who.

I am referred to as *Adyeeri*, an *Empaako* or nickname given by the Tooro tribe. A complicated cultural custom, simply put, it is one of only 14 names that the Tooro people receive in addition to their given name. Even small kids call their parents by their *Empaako*. When a local meets you, the first question is *"Empaako yawe?"* This begins the ritual of greeting. If someone doesn't ask my *Empaako*, they refer to me as Madam or Mama, even if they are as old as me. For an outsider to be given an *Empaako* is an honor. Unfortunately, tourists banter around, dubbing each other with an *Empaako* and laughing. The locals give each other a look and sigh. *Bzungu*, foreigners, are such strange people to most Ugandans.

I have been here a while, so I have picked up some speaking mannerisms which come across in my writing. For example, I will often use two words when a contraction might be more common. And the past and future tenses can get jumbled.

I am on a countdown for my remaining years on earth. I have tried to follow God's directions yet often messed up. I have no desire to retire and lie on a beach somewhere. I hope that God may give me more years and that I will be able to see YES Uganda continue to thrive. I pray that someone may be encouraged to come and assist in the ongoing success of our program.

I challenge all of my program graduates to evaluate their own lives and ask themselves, "What is my contribution to my people and the world at large?" I pray the young people who have benefited from the program will pass it forward in their own way and make a positive impact in their lives. My prayer is for YES Uganda to continue way beyond my years on earth and be a vessel of hope for young people here in Uganda.

I hope that people are encouraged by my story and realize that despite our flaws and mistakes, God is working through us. I hope you readers embrace your own unique superpower, believe in your own ability to be a positive force in the world, and see what amazing things God can do through his people.

Chapter 1

Unconventional Conviction

Normally, Highland Lake, Maine, has cool, temperate weather until the winter snows. The month I was born must have been foreshadowing my life today barely north of the equator in Uganda. The day I was born, Maine's hot air irritated my mother. She was sweating and uncomfortable well before the long labor and painful birth. In the years and decades to come, she found many more reasons to revile me. I entered her unhappy world on July 17, 1944.

I had two brothers and a sister. My sister Jean Elizabeth Adams was 10 years older than me. Later, she became Jean Leavy, her last married name. My brother Bill – William Henry Adams – was 6 years older, and Henry – Henry Alexander Adams III – was only 14 months older. I was the last child of Dorothy and Henry Alexander Adams Jr.

My memories of Highland Lake are vague. I remember living with no close neighbors, and if Henry and I heard a car coming we would run with excitement to wave as it passed by.

I remember fearing Mother right from the start. She was so unpredictable. In the morning, she might bake Henry and me cupcakes and by evening lose her temper, screaming and crying. In hindsight these many years later, I have come to realize that Mother most likely had some serious mental condition unrecognized back then, as well as a hard childhood herself. However, as a child I could not understand why she acted with such anger. We children tiptoed around, dreading we might make her angry.

Except for Jean. She would talk back to Mother, play tough and get into terrifying arguments. Jean gave me a mother's love even though she was just a kid. When I went to bed scared that Mother would enter in a tantrum, Jean would sing to me. I remember two Bing Crosby songs she sang first to me and later to her son Tommy. She would lean over my bed and sing *Swinging on a Star* and *Far Away Places*. She may have been trying to give us hope – that someday we'd escape Mother to fairy tale castles. How could she know her lullaby foreshadowed my own journey to Hawaii and later Uganda?

> *Far away places with strange sounding names*
> *Far away over the sea*
> *Those far away places with the strange*
> *sounding names are*
> *Calling, calling me*

When she left home at 18 and I was 8, my heart broke.

When I was about 4 years old, my family moved to Steep Falls, Maine. We owned a small general store close to our house. A railroad ran through town. We kids thought it great fun to run alongside, watch the long trains pass ahead and wave to the men on the caboose.

Mother hated the town and the store. She disliked the neighbors. She hated the church goers.

My father was distant but kind. A quiet man, he tried to stay out of Mother's tirades. He never became violent. Drinking was his increasing downfall. He was often sick.

I might have escaped Mother's baleful eye through school, except I was terribly shy and had a difficult time with simple things. When I was five, I was kicked out of kindergarten. My teacher told my parents that I was retarded and should not be in school.

"I can't believe I'm stuck with a retard," Mother said. Even then I knew to stay quiet. Jean, who was so grown-up at 15, would talk back to Mother, but I withdrew.

"Not even smart enough to speak up for yourself. Why can't you be more like Bill or Henry?" she ranted. Compared to me, Bill and Henry were way above average in school.

For a long time, I didn't talk or want to play with anyone. The quieter I became, the angrier Mother would get. "Retard" was my first label and shaped my belief in myself and my capabilities. Now we don't use that word as we know more about learning differences, and celebrate the many entrepreneurs, artists, celebrities, etc. who are open about being dyslexic or autistic or differently abled.

I enjoyed school because the teacher did not push me if I was scared. Mother told her I was retarded because of a difficult delivery when I was born. Jean told me Mother drank and smoked heavily during pregnancy. I have struggled with learning disabilities all my life and wonder if Mother's behavior had anything to do with it. I, personally, have no memories of her drinking.

Mother didn't need to drink to terrorize us. Shy of outright brutality, she would shake or slap us. She'd grab my arm so hard she'd leave bruises. My teacher alerted the school authorities, and they called Mother.

"She's so clumsy," Mother told them, smiling pleasantly if a bit chagrined. "Those are probably from her brother rescuing her from a fall. You know how kids are." To me, she shot the "Don't Say A Word" look. After that, she was scared to hit me. When she did lose control, she made sure to hit where bruises wouldn't show.

At times, I think Mother felt bad about treating us roughly. She would lavish attention on us. She would bake cookies and give us little parties. At Christmas and birthdays, she fussed over us and gave us loads of toys. We would be quite confused.

I learned early on how to stay out of trouble. I could tell when she was not in a right mood and knew that I needed to stay quiet and out of sight. When we had visitors, she always treated us wonderfully. We used our "Mother's company manners" and wished it could be real.

When I was six, I was enrolled in the town's one room schoolhouse. Children from grades one through six sat in rows in a downstairs room while 7th and 8th graders studied upstairs.

I learned about God in that small one room school.

Mother was an angry atheist. Dad, who would not argue with Mother, never said much. As a rather lost and scared child, I was thrilled to learn about a God who loved me. I accepted God into my life. I did not understand about Jesus or any of the concepts of Christianity, but God became real to me. I silently held on to Him from the start.

As I was learning about God, Jean decided that she also was a Christian.

"Christianity is for weak people who need a god who doesn't exist," Mother told Jean. "You're not bringing that nonsense into the house."

"I believe in God," said Jean. "Teacher gave us Bibles, and I'm keeping it."

"That Bible is trash," said Mother, grabbing it and throwing Jean's Bible into the fire.

Jean yelled and cried, but the harm was done. Henry, who was intelligent in school, took Mother's side.

I hid my Bible and again withdrew. I learned not to share my belief at all. God's message was too important to me, and I clung to God's love. God was closely with me in these hard times. I kept my Bible hidden, afraid of

Mother's anger, the huge arguments she and Jean had, of losing this precious gift.

When I think that, now, religion is not allowed in schools, I wonder if I would have learned about God's love. It makes me so sad to know that American kids no longer can be taught anything about God if their parents do not believe.

I remember loving big snowstorms. Once, we had to dig a tunnel from the door of our house to the store. After a storm, Jean would take us to a large hill on a toboggan. When Henry and I were only seven and six, Jean broke her arm when her toboggan ran into a tree. We managed to pull her all the way home through the snow.

We were poor, but we did not know that. Poverty was all we had ever known. We had some chickens for the eggs. I made pets out of them and gave them all names. They would follow me around and come to me if I called them.

Once I relaxed a bit, I started to learn. I loved learning to read. Math and writing were difficult. And while I slowly became a bit less shy with the neighboring kids, I still hardly talked.

Maybe it would have been better to stay away from them. I suffered from the whole gambit of childhood diseases and then some. Mumps, measles, whooping cough, scarlet fever plus had my tonsils removed. I've been plagued by illness one way or another. In some ways, my early illnesses may have made my body fragile (but then who doesn't ache in their 70s?!). In other ways, they prepared me to deal decades later with the many physical illnesses and challenges suffered by the children and people I love.

Once, I caught pneumonia. We lived far from any doctor or hospital, and we were in the middle of a winter storm. My parents managed to get a doctor on the phone. The doctor sent an ambulance, but on the way, it crashed on the slippery roads. The doctor then came for me in his own car. He held me in his lap as we drove to a hospital in Portland. I fell ill near Christmas, and in the hospital the nurses spoiled me. Everyone was so loving. I felt safe and did not want to go home.

Dr. Eppinger showed me so much love that I wished I could stay sick. I have few memories of names, but his name is burned into my mind.

Chapter 2

Refuge in Horses

When I was going to the third grade in 1952, we moved to Falmouth, Maine. Mother seemed happy to be going there. We had a pretty house near a river and forests and still close to the city of Portland where my dad worked at a bank.

Because we were getting older, Mother also took a job and left us home with instructions to do different jobs such as cleaning the house or weeding the garden and such.

That was very exciting for me. I loved the new home. I made some close friends.

Henry was not social and always tried to follow after me. Mother ordered me to let him. I resented it terribly.

I got on really well with Bill who I looked up to. He started reading at the age of 3 and built a radio at 6. He always got 100% in all school exams. However, he was socially unaccepted as people considered him abnormal and shied away from him. He used to play tricks on me, and we would race through the house chasing each other. When he was about 12 or 13, he made a car from 4 wheels, a frame and a motor he built. He nailed a chair to the wooden floorboard made from scavenged boards from the dump. I sat on the floorboards beside him, hanging on to handles he built for me to stay on. Way out in the countryside, he would fly around back roads while we screamed in laughter. Bill had a major electrical lab in our unfinished basement beside an ancient coal furnace. He showed me inventions such as lightning that would jump from post to post. I loved being part of his inventions and adventures. He was categorized as a genius while I was listed as a retard, but he constantly assured me that I might be different in my ability to learn but that I was NOT retarded. His encouragement was so, so important to me.

My years in Falmouth were the happiest of my childhood memories. I loved roaming the forests and playing by the river. I was happiest with animals. I knew that I was "different," but animals accepted me. If I sat still wild animals would come close. Squirrels and birds, even deer and once a moose came close.

I was doing better in school although math and numbers were difficult for me. I remained an average student no matter how hard I struggled. I still did not fit in with regular kids. My clothes were ragged. People did not approve of my parents.

I had a teacher who made me feel so guilty every Monday morning.

"Raise your hands if you went to church yesterday," she'd ask. I was the only one who did not go to church.

"Carol," she said, "Tell your mother that you want to attend church."

I'd just sit quietly until the class moved on. I would never say anything that might anger mother. Asking to go to church would certainly do that. I still had a strong faith, but I kept it to myself. I hid any thought or opinion that was important to me. That way, no one could take it away from me.

I have mixed memories of my years in Falmouth because my sister Jean fought constantly with Mother. Jean wanted to date, and Mother forbade it. This caused terrible screaming battles within the house, and Mother called Jean every terrible name possible. Jean was the most important person in my life. Hearing those terrible accusations hurt.

Jean became pregnant, made herself abort and almost died. Soon after her abortion, she met a young farmer and married him. Wally was a good man, but Jean could not settle down so easily. She had a baby---Tommy---but left Wally before the baby was even one year old.

Jean came back home with Tommy. Probably the biggest mistake she ever made. Jean had a night job as a waitress, and Mother constantly accused her of terrible misbehaviors. Mother decided to take Tommy back to the father and tell a judge that Jean was an unfit mother.

I will never forget the morning when Jean came home to find her baby gone and Mother screaming at her. Jean went to her room, threw her clothes in an old suitcase and got in her old pick-up truck. She drove out not knowing where she was headed. Her life is another story which I won't begin to get into. She had many adventures as well as eight husbands and died a sad alcoholic.

About three miles from our house there was a chicken farm and a pond. When I was about 11 years old, Henry, my best friend Barbie and I got jobs sorting eggs there, working for "Mr. F." We missed the worst of chicken farming, but even we had to deal with the heat, the feathers and dander in the air. Poultry dust is a mix of bird feed, bedding, droppings, old feathers and dander. When we finished for the day, we'd swim in the pond.

"I have a bad feeling about Mr. F," I once told Henry.

"This is better than going home," Henry said.

After I had been there for about four weeks, Mr. F came swimming with us. He drew near me and tried to fondle me underwater. I was terrified and resisted. He pulled me closer, rubbing against me.

"If you scream, I'll drown you," he said, pushing me beneath him.

I struggled with the advantage of being small and slippery in the water. I kneed him and swam away as fast as I could. I put Henry and Barbie between us and got out without saying a word.

I could not tell Mother because I knew she would blame me, and I thought maybe I was at fault. I know better now, but I didn›t even tell Henry.

Upset and confused, I quit the job.

"You're a lazy, stupid girl," Mother scolded, not for the first or last time. I would rather my mother call me "stupid and lazy" as opposed to all the terrible things I heard her call Jean. It was easier to just take her insults than to risk her knowing the truth and blaming me for it.

In 1957, when I was 13, my parents decided to leave Maine and move to a better area for my brother Henry's higher education. We moved to Skaneateles, New York, on the West side of Skaneateles Lake.

I was just entering junior high. I was scared about leaving my friends and school but excited also. My first days in school were difficult. I was welcomed by all the girls the first day, but I must not have passed their teen girls newcomers tests. My clothes were old. My father was not any important person. Skaneateles is a wealthy town, and a newcomer is an outsider for a long time.

The next day, I was alone and so terribly shy. I feared and hated school and dreamed of the day I would be free. As a young person, years seemed like an eternity. I slowly found my position and developed friendships with girls of similar backgrounds.

As I grew older, my relationship with Mother became more and more difficult. She did not approve of my friends, and there were many times when I felt she hated me. She would not permit normal friendships, no overnight visits with girlfriends. We were to come directly home from school. I couldn't go to football games or any school events.

My life was miserable, and I felt guilty about fearing to stand up to Mother and express my faith in God. That faith had continued to sustain me through a lonely and unhappy childhood, and I had learned much by reading my Bible in secret.

We lived on Hencoop Road, a country lane with beautiful views. The house was a flat roofed farmhouse with an old barn next to it. I had a secret desire to some-day own a horse, and I saw big possibilities in this place. By the time I was 16, I bought my first horse, a starved yearling I named Ballerina. I knew very little about horse training but was gifted with all animals. Ballerina and I learned together as she grew. I joined a 4H horse club and finally started coming out of my terrible shy-ness. I had found something I could succeed in. For the first time in my life, I felt confident and good at something. It took all those years of isolation to come into my unique ability with animals, especially horses. I felt out of place among most people, but always felt at home and accepted by animals.

My mother took an interest in my activities. She encouraged me to get more horses. I slowly acquired a starved gelding, an albino slightly crazy horse, and a black half Morgan/thoroughbred. As I look back on all of this, I see my love for my horses and Mother's rare approval held me in Skaneateles as my siblings were leaving. I loved the lake being so close, and I enjoyed farm life.

We bought a tractor that I learned to use and helped with clearing the steep driveway of snow. Deadly beautiful, Skaneateles huge snows and cold winters were often a challenge. I still shudder when I remember crawling under the house in a small space with a blow torch to thaw out water pipes.

"Henry should help," I dared complain.

"Housework and repairs are yours," Mother said, ignoring my fear.

Mother had become more and more disturbed and angry.

"Please," I asked.

"Henry's smart. He needs to study," she said. "You're stupid. At least you can be useful."

One evening, as Henry drove up our road with Mother, the sun blinded him. He did not see the farm truck parked on the side of the road. He drove the passenger side right under the high truck bed. The bed of the truck came into the car and smashed Mother's head badly. Henry was unhurt. Mother was rushed to the hospital by ambulance.

My guilty feelings increased intensely as I kept wishing she might die. I knew that was wrong, but by then my life was miserable a good deal of the time. With Mother in the hospital, Dad relaxed, and we enjoyed his being around. Dad was an alcoholic. I often tried to protect him and hide his bottles if he forgot and left them someplace where Mother would find them.

Mother did recover. She seemed to come home angrier, if that was possible.

Dad was drinking more and more.

Jean was in and out of our lives. She and I kept

in touch through a friend who snuck letters to me and mailed letters out.

Bill was out and married to a divorced lady who had two kids. He had one boy, Dylan with her. He then left her and took a black lady who he moved in with. She had 6 kids, and he had two more with her. His life became hectic, but like Jean, I won't get into that either.

By 1962, I had graduated from high school and became a minor success in the local horse shows. With some money my grandparents willed me, I made the huge and foolish mistake of building up a horse business on the family farm. Mother was completely in favor. She had become possessive of me, and with the other kids gone from home she feared that I might also leave her.

I designed my dream barn with an indoor arena so I could train and teach riding year-round. I knew nothing about construction and did not realize the contractor cut many corners. The exterior and roof was finished in January of 1963. During a wild and windy storm, I went into the barn and saw that the southern end wall was moving with the wind gusts. When I phoned the contractor, he laughed and said all buildings have a certain amount of give and take in a storm. About 5 minutes later, I heard a huge sound like an airplane crash. The whole barn had blown down with the large roof completely upside down.

My dream was in a mess. If I had been more mature, I would have left the family land. Yet I stayed. I hired a lawyer to fight the contractor over his poor work in constructing my barn. It was a frustrating and dragged-out process. I managed doing odd jobs for some of the local horse owners.

One day, my dad disappeared. I was home alone with my mother who was more and more angry and paranoid and sometimes delusional. He had left on an ocean liner but ended up in psychiatric care somewhere in Europe. He returned and begged Mother to take him back. He swore that he was now fine.

Finally, my stable was re-built. I started building a successful horse training and boarding business as well as teaching riding. I had horse shows on the home property. My students and I attended horse shows almost weekly.

My mother loved horse shows and lived for them. She also held on to me tighter than ever. She did not want me to make friends. She often was angry. I was always embarrassed when I did not win or place in a high position because she would loudly proclaim how stupid or corrupt the judge was.

Dad would stay home, always willing to handle the chore of feeding the horses left behind in the stable. I loved him, and we got along well. Even that incurred Mother's wrath, so we learned mostly to stay quiet. By then, I had become quite good at handling Mother, but it was a tiring, never ending task.

Chapter 3

Dad and The Bank

One evening in September of 1966, Dad came to me in the kitchen where I was washing dishes after supper.

"Carol", he said, "I can't stand my life."

"What do you mean?" I asked. I knew what he would say.

"I can't continue living this way, living with your mother," he answered.

I didn't know what to say. Everyone else had left.

"What are you going to do?" I'm still bewildered by his reply.

"Tomorrow, I'm going to rob the bank."

"Don't be ridiculous Dad, you know you won't do that," I told him, getting angry. I was also in a bad situation, working to keep Mother's behavior under control in public.

He looked hurt.

"I am sorry for any trouble this will cause you. I love you," he said quietly, and he walked out.

The next evening when Dad did not come home, I felt sick. I knew what he had done. I went into his room where I found a suitcase missing and a note saying that he was going to visit his brother John for the weekend. My mother believed this and was angry that he ran off without telling us in person. I knew different and spent a long and terrible weekend with no one to tell what I knew. I considered phoning the police. Perhaps Dad would be caught and get a light punishment, but there was no way that I would do that to him.

About mid-day on Monday, an official looking car drove up our driveway -- the FBI. Mother, of course, knew nothing. I also pretended not to know what was happening. This really set Mother off in total hysteria while the FBI tore apart our house. Doing my regular work of teaching riding and feeding and caring for the horses had to continue throughout the long, difficult afternoon.

That night, the 6 p.m. news showed pictures of Dad. They reported him embezzling $95,500 dollars from the bank.

I went to bed before the 10 p.m. news, and there a miracle occurred that I will never forget. I was in bed feeling destroyed and hopeless and guilty and scared and many emotions I could not even pray about. I was keeping my head in the pillow so that Mother would not hear my sobs. Suddenly, I knew that someone was in the room and had his hand on my shoulder. The room was very bright and a love and understanding and a message---not verbal--- that all would be OK and that He was with me filled the room. I did not want to move or even breathe and wanted the sensation of such total love to never leave. I ended up falling asleep in complete peace and woke up knowing that things would be hard, but that God was close.

Things certainly were not easy. Mother was out of control. Everyone would stop talking when I walked into a store in our small town. Many phoned to say how sorry they were but mostly wanted to get direct information that they could gossip to others. A rude FBI agent visited many times. Students were pulled from my classes by mothers who did not want their kids associating with me. As these things go, the talk slowed down, and I continued running my stable and horse shows and such.

January 31, 1967, the FBI caught Dad. Again, gossip and news flared for some time and then died down.

I still regret not attending his trial. I didn't visit when he was in the Auburn prison. I was too weak to confront Mother.

Dad pled guilty and went to Danbury Prison in Connecticut. There he was happy and accepted Christ as his personal Savior under a prison ministry. He was paroled sooner than he wanted and begged to come home. He was a broken man. Mother had no room to forgive anything. The last time I saw him was at the New York State Fair where we met in secret.

About a year and a half later, Mother bluntly broke the news.

"You father is dead," she said.

I was stunned and stood there saying nothing.

"Well, I'm not spending a dime on him," she said. "I'm not paying to have that useless man buried."

"What will you do?" I asked.

"He killed himself, so he doesn't deserve anything from me. I'm going to donate his body to some medical school to pick apart his flesh."

My father wasn't buried, but I buried my grief deeply and continued with life.

I continued horse training, teaching riding, attending horse shows and leading a 4-H horse club. My riding garnered many awards, including New York State champion showman for 4-H. The stable was always full and so were the lesson schedules. I managed all aspects of the stable including repairs, feeding the animals, keeping the stalls clean, running the tractor and manure spreader, as well as putting on horse shows and attending others and occasionally judging shows.

Mother loved the horse shows and lived her life through me. I began to believe that she could not survive if I did not take care of her. She did not even drive a car. I took her shopping and other places she wanted to go.

Early one spring, a horse fell on me and broke my ankle badly. I was hospitalized for many days. Some of my older students took over the care of the stable and checked on Mother. She grew angry at me for being hurt and upset that I could not drive her places when I got out because I had a full leg cast.

The leg slowly healed but not my emotions. As Mother got worse, she would hurt herself to keep me from going out. She fell and broke her arm when I was not home and made quite a lot of fuss that it was my fault. She even started cutting her arms, overdosing on medicines and doing serious harm to herself if I left her for even a few hours.

At night, she often would wake me up in a panic telling me that someone was sneaking around outside. I pretended to go and chase someone away then tell her that the person got scared and ran. She slept with a large knife. One night she was sneaking around, thinking someone was outside. I had gotten up for some reason and walked into the room she was hiding in. She almost struck me with the knife. When she applied for a gun permit, I put in a word that she was not stable, and the permit was denied.

My health deteriorated. A doctor said that I had something called Lupus and that I should rest a lot. I hired a lady to do some of the feeding and heavy cleaning of the stables.

I needed a personal life, but that was impossible with Mother. I dated a few times. I met a divorced man with six kids who I started seeing. Mother became frantic and screamed and cried if I went out with him. This made my time with him seem tense, but I still cared deeply for him.

"Mother, John asked to go to a concert. You'll be on

your own for a few hours tonight." I said one evening.

"No, you can't," she said.

"It's OK," I tried to reason. "I need a break. Everything will be fine."

"You're a horrible daughter, leaving me here to die, to be raped or worse."

"No one is going to hurt you," I said, determined to take some time off. I'd had enough and was ready to snap myself. I'd been thinking it was time to leave my home entirely.

"If you leave, I'll kill myself," she threatened.

"That's your decision," I said, and left. I'd had enough of her histrionics.

When I returned home, the house was still. She didn't greet me at the door screaming. I gingerly walked in. Perhaps she'd exhausted herself and fallen asleep.

When I entered the living room, she was lying dead on the living room floor, pretending. No one would die so dramatically posed. I could see her breathing. I looked at her and went to bed. Later, I heard her go to bed.

Another drama passed, I thought.

In the morning, after checking with the lady feeding the horses, I came back for a cup of coffee.

"You're a horrible daughter, ungrateful," Mother started screaming. "You'd rather whore around than be respectful."

I tried to calm her.

She grabbed a cup and threw it at me. Then another, and anything she could grab. All the while yelling every hateful thought she'd ever had.

Something broke in me.

"I can't take this anymore," I said. "I'm leaving."

"You can't leave," she ranted. "Where would you go? Who would take trash like you? You can't leave me. What will I do?"

"Guess you'll have to take care of yourself," I said.

That rainy Saturday morning, I headed away down the road on foot, not knowing where to go or what to do. I just knew I had to go. This was the first of many times I would have to leave all I own and all I know to find a place to just exist. It became a consistent theme on my unique journey to freedom.

A neighbor saw me walking and called me to come in. She settled me in a room alone to try and think. While in prayer and tears, I remembered a lady who ran a stable and a home for delinquent teenage boys. I phoned her and asked if she could use live in help. She said that she would love to have me and drove over and picked me up. I have always felt at home with other people who have been discarded by society, and the thought of sharing my love for horses with orphaned boys was so exciting to me.

On August 17, 1974, 30 years old, I finally left home.

Chapter 4

Find Your Tribe

I believe God chose to train me and prepare me for eventual service to Him during the next few years.

Mary and Vern Statzer cared for delinquent kids. I arrived on a rainy Saturday afternoon to a large three-story farmhouse. The kids were all curious but a bit shy. They stood back and watched. I stayed in a room at the peak of the roof with a round window that looked down to the front lawn. The property had a pond and a waterfall that used to power a grinding mill.

Mary's husband Vern said very little. They had three children of their own, a baby girl, a 5-year-old boy and a 6-year-old girl. Mary was outgoing and full of laughs and jokes all the time. The family hosted 12 to 15 kids. We ate at a large picnic table where heaps of food were served.

My first emotions were elation and freedom. For the first time in my life, I was making decisions for myself.

I felt a bit overwhelmed as well. I immediately involved myself in the stable and the home and made myself busy trying to improve conditions for the horses. They had saddle sores and were underfed.

After about a week, my brother Henry came from Colorado to see what could be done.

"You have to go back home," he tried to convince me.

"I can't do it anymore," I said.

"She needs you," he said. "That's your place."

"Really?" I asked, angry. "Well, I think it's past time for you and Bill to take over."

"That's ridiculous," he said.

"I'm not giving up my freedom," I said, decisively. My relationship with Mother was trashed and the one with my brothers might never recover, but I couldn't go back.

Henry ended up taking Mother back with him to Colorado. He couldn't manage more than 3 months before he sent her back to Skaneateles.

Leaving the farm that I had grown up on and developed into a successful business was the most painful decision I've ever made. Many people judged me harshly for leaving Mother while others closer to the situation understood completely. Losing my stable and all that went with it was the hardest time of my life. Being thrown in with delinquent teens in a foster home was in a weird way helpful. They were terribly misused and abandoned kids who I felt truly needed my help. I couldn't feel sorry for myself for too long knowing their situations, and I was just happy to be there for them.

I retrieved my camper pickup truck and my horse trailer from our farm, loading my photos, horse show trophies and ribbons and my riding clothes. The boarding horses were gone, and I brought my own three horses to the Statzer farm.

I went out a couple more times with the man with the six kids. He was feeling quite poorly and weak. I convinced him to see a doctor. He was diagnosed with leukemia and was hospitalized. His ex-wife came back on the scene, and he died within a month.

The summer days filled with work at the riding stable and with the boys. I got on well with these discarded kids who were mostly just boys who never had a fair chance in the world. I taught them how to handle and ride the horses and watched as they developed more and more self-confidence.

Despite my contribution, I learned early on that all was far from good at this home. Both the foster parents were heavy drinkers. Their own three small children were badly neglected. The boys were treated harshly. Even so, the boys begged me not to bring in the authorities because the next home could be worse.

I also learned quite early that Mary was a lesbian. I had lived a sheltered life while caring for Mother, and I was shocked. Mary would try to force herself on me while drunk, and I'd fend her off. While sober, she tried to convince me that I would enjoy that lifestyle, but it horrified me. I had never known a gay person in my thirty years of life.

Mary and Vern bought food for the boys from a blind mafia man who sold food from behind an abandoned service station. The food was outdated and sometimes the meat had gone bad. The man also ran a bookie service and had a wall of phones ringing nonstop. Mary brought me with her one time. He demanded in harsh tones to know who I was. The same man owned several buildings in a slum district of Syracuse and had several of them burn down at the loss of many lives. He was a scary person.

One normal person involved with the family was an elderly aunt. She loved the little ones dearly and was concerned about them.

Despite room and board, I needed to earn some salary. I learned to drive a school bus and started driving for a city school with a 60-passenger bus.

Mary owned a Standardbred stallion she wanted trained for harness racing. We took him to the Syracuse fairgrounds where I started working with him in a sulky. I knew nothing about harness racing, but Mary felt that if he was fast, he would be worth a lot of money. Young enough to be overconfident, I started training him.

I was soon befriended by an older Italian man. He made sure no one hassled me as there were few ladies working the track. In my naivety, I did not realize he was another mafia man who everyone feared. So much was happening over such a short time frame for me, and he taught me so much.

I still believed I had Lupus and would not live long. I drank a fair amount of beer and some harder stuff but tried to keep it under control. The buzz I would get helped me leave bad memories behind for a bit. Alcohol provided a rare comfort for me, and I leaned on it from time to time.

We headed into winter. I worked hard with a chainsaw, cutting trees and building shelters for the horses on the hillsides. We brought our stallion home from the fairgrounds for the winter. I continued driving the school bus.

Another bus driver, Holly, started taking me out some evenings to local restaurants and country and western music bars. I enjoyed this immensely until I learned Holly was a married man. He told me that his wife did not love him anymore----again how stupid I was. I continued to see him off and on.

Christmas was coming and my heart broke for the boys who had no one. Mary drank a lot more, and Vern was often not there at all. I managed the stable and the small kids. I will never forget that Christmas Eve. I told the boys that I would take them to a midnight mass. They all found the best clothes they owned, and I headed out with 12 ragged boys along with the two small kids leaving only the baby home. We made quite a sight heading into the large Catholic church that evening, but the boys loved it. I didn't know much about Catholic worship. As we walked down the aisle, I admired the beautiful decorations along the ceiling and walls, not looking ahead. The man in front of me stopped to kneel before entering the pew and I fell on top of him, completely flattening him. I know how to make a grand appearance!

We arrived home to a surprise -- a large bunch of gifts left by some good Samaritan group from town. We had a great time. My heart was so full watching the boys open their gifts. Their smiles were electric!

During the harsh winter, my small round window rattled in the wind, and snow worked in around it. The big old house was never warm enough. The kids constantly had colds and runny noses. Vern and Mary increased drinking, adding to the pervasive tension. The early mornings were hard to get out of the bed and drive to the school bus station. I had to do a complete check of the bus and often wash it after doing two runs, one for high school and one for elementary school. Between bus runs, I cleaned the stable and cared for the horses. Taking our racing stallion into town pulling a sleigh with bells was the highlight. I would sometimes bring little Becky to school in the sleigh.

My soul welcomed being my own person even though I left everything behind and had absolutely no money. Mother closed out our joint bank account soon after I left. When Mother returned from Henry's, she took my cats out in the car and threw them out a window. She sold all the furniture and possessions in the house including inherited pieces from Dad's parents. In the winter, she sold the farm leaving me nothing at all. She was determined to be as hurtful as possible to punish me for leaving. Dad had left the farm in my name, but the laws of New York state gave the surviving wife all property. I was in no emotional state to take Mother to court.

Early in the spring, we brought the stallion back to the racetrack, hoping to sell him as a racehorse at a good price. Taking him on the track with the wind and mud in my face while sitting with my legs almost stretched to his hindquarters as they reached for the stirrups was exciting and sometimes dangerous work. It was exhilarating to feel as one with such a powerful, magnificent creature. It was as if I was flying weightlessly with him around the track. He was a well-mannered animal but not racing quality. The trips around the track felt fast to me, but some of the things I overheard being said about us made me realize we were a joke.

One nice spring morning during the school Easter break, Vern suggested I take the boys to the track to watch me work out the stallion. This seemed unusual as he never cared about the boys. However, the boys loved the excitement and had a wonderful time. They got on well with the other trainers and some of them had hopes to get part time jobs for the summer with the racehorses. We headed back in the late afternoon in high spirits with a hint of spring in the air and much laughter and foolishness coming from the back of the car. I felt good, thinking what good therapy this had been for the boys. Horses are so healing.

While driving back to the house, I started to consider what I wanted for my future. I knew I couldn't stay where I was and that I needed to make some plans. I sure did not know my future was being changed even as I drove!

As we approached the house, we all saw heavy smoke

and the old farmhouse in complete flames. We pulled off the road just down from the house and ran the rest of the way to the farm. The firemen were still working on the house, which was an obvious total loss. They were dousing the barn to keep it from catching fire. The boys and I turned all the horses out just in case the barn went up. We drove them to some higher pastures. No words can express the feeling of seeing the house burning down. "Here we go again," I thought. In my pursuit of peace, I lose every single thing I own. Again. All I possessed was in my third-floor room. Pictures, books, trophies and ribbons from years of showing horses and many other things with emotional value. As I stood there, I knew this fire was not an accident. A feeling of loss, anger and despair overcame me as I watched.

That evening, the welfare department took the boys to different homes. They left amidst tears and hugs. The next-door neighbor took in Mary, Vern, me and their 3 kids. We slept on the floor on mattresses. Vern acted excited and happy. He talked about the new home he planned on building with the large insurance policy he had taken out a month before. I fed and cared for the horses in a daze. I bought some underwear and clothes for myself as I only had what I'd worn to the track the day before.

Two days later, the grown daughter of the family who bought my family's farm called me. Her family asked me to manage the stable and handle the riding lessons at the very stable I had built myself years ago. I was ecstatic!

Chapter 5

Control is an Illusion

The day I left the Statzer's, I had a huge row with Vern, telling him I knew he burned the house down. By then, we were living in a house trailer that they moved on to the property. I threw what little I had in my truck and headed back to Skaneateles and my farm.

I left my truck with Holly who was borrowing a neighbor's tools to make some repairs on my camper. I walked the last bit to my old home, with a sense of hope and belonging. I'd always dreaded approaching home, never knowing what mood I'd find Mother. This time I returned knowing I'd have more control.

The family invited me to dinner.

"Thank you for having me," I said, sitting at the table. "I'm excited to get back to work."

The family looked uncomfortable.

"Well, about that," said the father, "I've been reconsidering."

I stopped serving my plate, the familiar dread returned. Control is an illusion.

"I've decided I don't want you here," he said. "Too awkward, this isn't your home anymore. Don't want to confuse things."

"Uhm, I don't want you uncomfortable." My brain scrambled for a solution. "I'll find a place nearby."

"Won't work," he said, pointedly looking at his daughter. "Don't want to reopen a horse business here."

No one at the table said anything on my behalf. And, what could I say? They were all strangers in my home, but it was no longer my home. I couldn't force them to take me on, to care for my beloved horses. The father's word was final.

I barely remember that supper. I tried to be pleasant, to hold it together, but I couldn't swallow my food. I left as soon as I could. I ran down the road to my truck and climbed into the camper shaking.

"Just drive away," I told Holly when he checked on me.

"What happened?" he asked.

"I need to get drunk," I said, barely coherent.

"Tell me what's going on," he said.

The neighbor had come out, hearing my hysterics.

"They don't want me," I sobbed. "Nothing ever works. I need a damn drink!"

"Get a grip, Carol," Holly said harshly. The neighbor nodded with him, none too friendly.

"Get a grip, that's your answer? You get to go back to your wife. What about me?"

Holly and the neighbor chided me for letting my emotions get out of control. Told me to grow up. Everything they said made me feel worse. Why does being different mean being unlovable?

I had a bottle of codeine in my purse that I kept for migraines. I grabbed the bottle and took a handful. I just wanted oblivion at that moment. I do not think I was considering suicide. I just wanted to know nothing for the time.

"What are you doing? Are you crazy?" both men started yelling, grabbing for me.

I jumped out of the truck and took off across the fields in the dark. While at a blind run, I ran into a barbed wire electric fence. The shock paralyzed me while electricity coursed through my body.

The men found me and pulled me off the fence. Together they carried me to the truck where they locked me in the back. Holly drove me to the hospital. In the emergency room, I was treated harshly and then put in a psychiatric ward.

My legs were quite painful from the barbed wire. My stomach was sore from being made to vomit. Shame made this the lowest time in my life.

The next morning, I checked myself out. Holly came to get me, but made it clear he, too, was ashamed of me. I did not know where to go. I couldn't go back to Vern. I had little money. Holly talked me into going away to Canada for the weekend to relax, but I couldn't.

When we returned from Canada, I dropped him off at his home.

"I'll find my own way," I said, speeding off.

I drove around aimlessly. I found different places to park my truck, and I started living from the back. The small camper had a bed. I found public showers in different places and never stayed in the same place twice. Often, I parked illegally, and I spent the nights scared.

I was still driving a school bus, starting to avoid Holly. In all my troubles, I knew being with a married man was wrong. I had basically been using him because he was friendly and I was feeling quite lost, sick and unsure of what to do next.

I contacted a family who had a daughter that I had taught riding and asked if I could stay with them for a few weeks until I knew my next steps in life. I was told rather rudely that they did not wish me to be there. I had considered several other possible places, but that reaction made me hesitate to call anyone else. Nobody wanted me.

After about two weeks, I saw a family who used to bring their boys for riding lessons back on my farm. Sally and Grant Olcott knew about the fire and asked me where I was living. When I told them that I was living in my truck, they insisted that I move in with them. I accepted gladly and gratefully moved my horses to their small stable.

To this day, I still consider them a real family to me.

One of the first things I did was tell them about my lupus. From reading the dictionary and research at the library, I learned lupus is a progressive disease. They set me up with a good doctor who put me in a hospital and ran many tests. The doctor diagnosed severe anemia. Anemia, along with my emotional problems, caused my symptoms. With proper medical care, I recovered.

With summer school holiday approaching, I considered what my next step in my life should be. The Olcott's had four boys as well as the grandparents all in a small house. I couldn't stay with them. I found a part time job teaching riding at a stable some distance away. The small salary gave me some money to share for the food I ate.

I finally broke with Holly. He became furious. He said that if he could not have me no one could. Determined to make the break, I went to his house to tell him in front of his wife. I told her how sorry I was that I had been seeing her husband and how bad I felt. I promised I would stop seeing him. He stood right there while I talked with her. She was kind and seemed to understand that I had been lonely and grasping for friendship.

About a week later, Holly's wife phoned me from her home.

"He left here acting crazy," she said. "He says he's going to kill you."

That same afternoon, he came to the house where I was staying.

"I just want to talk," he said, sounding nicer than he ever had before.

"I don't think that's a good idea," I said, remembering

my promise to his wife.

"Come on, Carol, I don't want us to part with such harsh feelings" he said, sounding sincere.

I conceded, getting into his car to talk with him. He immediately changed. He sped away and started talking crazy.

"Stop!" I yelled, "let me out!"

He kept speeding.

We came up on a slow-moving tractor, forcing him to slow. Before he could pass, I jumped out. I ran to the nearest house.

"Call the police," I begged as Holly came running up.

I was afraid he would hurt the family, so ducked past him and started running down the road. He grabbed me and dragged me back into the car, racing off. Again, he was forced to slow, and I again jumped onto the gravel, scraping my arms and legs, running as fast as I could. Just as he was about to give chase, a police car came flying down the road. Holly took off.

I didn't check if the police caught him. I didn't want them to know about me. I hoped the affair was finished.

Two nights later, leaving the stable where I taught, I headed home on a back road. Just before dark, I saw Holly in his car waiting for me to pass by. I sped up as fast as I could. In the rearview mirror, I saw he pointed a gun out his window. His car was faster than my truck. We raced down an empty road, no houses, for about five miles. I was terrified. I decided to slam on my brakes. My pickup truck had a strong back metal bumper. I braced myself. His car crashed hard into the back of my truck and pushed us some way and almost sideways in the road. Without checking what damage I'd done him; I quickly straightened around and drove away. He never appeared in my rearview mirror, and I never saw him again.

I shared my experience with Holly with my racetrack mafia friend. About two months later, I learned Holly died of a heart attack. I did always worry that my mafia friend might have had something to do with Holly's death, but that chapter in my life was closed.

Early that summer, I flew to Alaska to visit my sister.

My very first time in an airplane -- what an adventure it was! Jean and her then husband Jack met me at the airport. We drove to the bar where Jack worked. Right away I saw that they both were heavy drinkers.

We toured Alaska. I had a great time and saw so many beautiful sights. Unfortunately. their continuous drinking dampened the experience. They started early in the morning and continued throughout each day. I often took over the driving because I did not feel safe with either of them behind the wheel.

I enjoyed the trip, but I was glad to return to NY and the Olcott family. I had gone on the trip with the thought that perhaps I could start a new life in Alaska, but soon realized I did not belong there.

On my return, I found that the Statzers were being investigated for arson and had disappeared. I worried about the twelve horses left behind. I drove there to find the ones in the stable had been several days without water or care. The horses in the pasture at least could fend for themselves a bit. I immediately got on the phone and called people who I felt would take care of the horses. With a friend, I trailered horses out all night to good homes. I still laugh when I remember giving all of Vern's horses away in the dead of night while the local police turned a blind eye.

I had many a late evening discussion with the Olcotts and their older boys. The oldest, Grant Jr., was finishing high school and wanted to be a professional trainer. They asked me to stay with them while they built a large indoor training arena and bought land nearby. I started school bus driving closer to where we lived.

I loved the family and the land. For the first time in some years, I felt some peace about my life. The Olcotts were strong Christians who attended a Methodist Church in the town. I attended with them on Sundays. After a few months, I met with the Reverend to get some serious spiritual advice. I had not made any firm commitment since leaving my mother concerning my spiritual life. I had attended different churches but always slid out before closing to avoid any questions. I was confused and felt guilty and even frightened.

Reverend John Fulton was wonderful. After several counseling sessions, I was baptized and joined the church as a member. That was April 11, 1976. I felt an overwhelming joy and acceptance from God. I finally belonged and could honestly call myself a Christian. I had loved the Lord since childhood but had never had the courage to oppose Mother concerning my belief. I felt guilt about hiding my faith that I carried even after leaving the family farm. I now was completely free!!!

The arena was built; we had horses boarded, and I was giving lessons. Life felt good yet there was tension in the air. Grant, Jr., had romantic ideas about running a horse stable but was a bit lazy. He didn't want the work that went with horses. Meanwhile, the father was not doing well and was perhaps depressed. We headed into winter struggling to make ends meet. The grandparents were elderly and difficult with the grandmother needing full time care.

One morning, I had come into the house and gone up to my room when I heard the parents talking downstairs.

"I want to leave NY," Grant said.

Sally must have made some quiet opposition.

"We need to start a new life," he answered.

"Where would we go?" Sally asked.

"Oklahoma," he said.

Right then and there, God put it into my mind that I needed a completely new start in some vastly different place. Part of my individual experience is constantly starting over. With my new spiritual freedom, I just knew that I no longer needed to amble along the periphery of other people's lives. For the first time, with my faith, I knew that I was enough on my own.

Chapter 6

Hot and Cold in Hawaii

I went downstairs.

"Heard us talking?" Sally asked on seeing me.

"I did," I said.

"You're still part of our family," Sally said.

"You're welcome to come with us to Oklahoma," Grant added.

"Thank you," I said with all sincerity, "but I'm moving to Hawaii."

"What?!" said Grant.

"Do you know anyone in Hawaii?" Sally asked with concern.

"No, nobody," I answered, "I don't even know much about the state."

I knew I'd taken a rather radical leap, but my mind was made up. I found library books and started planning my move. I sold and gave away my three horses and equipment.

In March of 1977, I was on a plane bound for Hawaii!!!

My luggage missed the flight. I arrived late afternoon after fourteen hours of flight and who knows how many hours in airports. I planned to find an inexpensive hotel......Not possible in Honolulu during peak tourist season.

"Do you know where I can stay a few days," I asked the young man behind the lost luggage counter.

"You came on vacation without making hotel reservations?" he asked.

"I'm not on vacation," I told him. "I came here to live."

"You don't look like 'one of them'," he said. I later learned he meant a hippy type.

He found me a cheap room right on Waikiki Beach. Scary with crowds of people, sirens wailing, everything felt overwhelming. When my luggage finally arrived, I decided to try a different island.

Reaching what seemed like a much smaller Maui was a relief. Palm trees brushed glass domes inside the terminal. Private jets parked under shade trees on the runway. Cars in the parking lot were strapped down with surf boards.

I bought a newspaper, looking for rentals with no success. I had a phone number a friend had given me for her mom, another Carol. The mother had married a Hawaiian man and lived somewhere on the island. When I phoned her, she told me to sit tight, and she'd get me.

Though a huge relief, I was determined that I would NOT become dependent and would find someplace to live as soon as possible. I was determined to forge my own path, as grateful as I was for the kindness of strangers, I had to make it on my own.

Carol drove me to Haiku where she lived in a cute cottage with her husband who was a leper. She had not told me, so my first sight of him was startling. His nose and lips were gone, and his fingers and feet were deformed. I quickly got past his appearance. An outgoing and intelligent man, I found myself at home with him right away. I have always felt at home with the outcasts.

I loved Haiku and learned as much as possible about the island. Until I knew a bit more about my future, I bought a motorcycle instead of a car. I thought it would be easy to drive since I knew how to ride a bike. I had some close calls as I learned to manage curving mountain roads. God had His angels working overtime taking care of me during my riding days.

Needing a job as soon as possible, I read that a chicken farm sought someone to collect and grade eggs. Ugh, another chicken farm. Well, at least Mr. F wouldn't be at this one. I got on my new bike and headed up the hill to apply. The man was surprised to see a *haole* (non-Hawaiian or not local person), but he told me to start in the morning.

Heading back to Carol's, I was at the 4-way intersection in Makawao, a rural town on the side of a mountain, east of Maui, when my bike stalled. I kept giving it gas from the handlebar and then let up the clutch on the other handle. I did not coordinate that well, and the bike reared up. I went all the way through the intersection on the back wheel before I realized that I had to give it less gas to make it come down. As it came down, I saw a flashing blue light coming after me -- the Maui police.

"What do you think you're doing?" asked the tall officer with a Polish name on his uniform when I pulled over.

"I wasn't showing off," I answered as nicely as I could, breathless. "I'm learning how to handle the bike."

"Oh really," he said sarcastically. "Maybe you should go back to where you came from."

"I just moved here," I explained.

"Maui doesn't need your type," he replied.

"I don't think you're Hawaiian either," I said, staring at his name tag.

Being mouthy to police in a strange place is NOT smart, and I headed out with a $50 dollar ticket.

The next day, I started collecting eggs alongside Hawaiian ladies who talked fast and with such an accent I thought they were speaking a different language. The farm had six houses with 10,000 hens in a house. We had to push carts with our legs and collect eggs as fast as we could and pile them on flats of 30 eggs, five flats high and six piles of flats to a cart. We then pushed the carts out and loaded them on pickup trucks and started again. I could swear after a time that the chickens were saying "Caaarrrooollll" with their vocalizations.

After hours of gathering eggs, we moved into the cleaning and sorting houses where the eggs were washed and sent through holes to size them and then packed into crates for shipping. The work was exhausting. At lunch time, a Hawaiian lady started talking with me and befriended me. The others were suspicious of this *haole* at their place.

The owner came up behind me while I was sorting eggs and reached around me and grabbed my breasts. I wore cowboy boots back then, and he wore rubber sandals. I took a quick step back on to his toes and stomped hard. He screamed and jumped away. I kept sorting. No more was said, and he never came near me again. I won the women's friendships that afternoon.

With chicken lice eating me alive, my job at the egg farm did not last long. However, it opened a lasting and deep friendship with Elizabeth Kaiama. I had rented a room from a couple I realized were dealing drugs from the house. I was not comfortable with them or their friends. Elizabeth invited me to spend time and even sleep over at her house with her six kids and her husband. I felt a true friendship with the whole Kaiama family. Peter, the husband, drove me around the island and taught me about the culture, people, and places.

My next job was at the airport as a security guard. Not too huge of a change as chickens wandered around. I held several different positions from checking the luggage going through the scanner to watching the luggage as people came to pick it up. One funny memory is the time I found a suitcase making buzzing and vibrating noises on the rack. I called in the armed guards. They in turn called the bomb squad. Everyone stood way back while men in what looked like space suits came to examine the case. As everyone held their breath and watched, a man called out that it was his suitcase. "I don't have anything dangerous in it," he said. He went right up to the case, opening it, to discover a battery-operated shaver had turned on inside. I got angry when the boss of the security company scolded me for causing so much trouble. Easy to say after he knew what was making the noise.

I left the airport security to do security at Kaahumanu shopping mall, easier than the loud and hectic airport. I found this position much better as the constant noise at the airport gave me severe headaches. The shopping mall was mostly boring but gave me time to meet people and window shop. After a while, my manager asked if I would take over full management of Wakenhut Security there on Maui. The office was in the city of Wailuku, just beyond where I already worked. I took it thinking a 9-to-5 office job would be easier….. It was NOT!

Life continued well, and I made more friends in the area. I was especially happy when Hawaiian people became close friends. The physical beauty and different cultures were wonderful. I didn't hang out only with *haoles*—white people—but mixed with many cultures and loved it. I joined the Po'okela Church in Makawao, a non-denominational protestant church. At the time, the pastor was a retired missionary from Samoa. Reverend Leslie Blomerly was wonderful and a strong Bible teacher. He helped strengthen my faith and understanding of the Bible. I got to know people from many different races in that church as well as on the Island. In hindsight, I see Maui as a training ground for Uganda. Here began my understanding of nationalities and cultures outside my experiences in small town New England.

I tried to get a job at the horse center, the largest stable on the Island, but they did not welcome outsiders. The matron of the stable did however allow me to form a 4-H horse club for Maui youth and use her facilities. I started getting to know some of the horse people in Maui.

I also worked for a couple of months for a Portuguese rancher in Makawao training one of his horses. While there, I met a Chinese man who owned Arabian horses way up on the mountain. He also asked me to do some training. These extra jobs with horses as well as my security job kept me busy and helped me meet some very nice people.

Pastor Blomerly asked me to stay at his house by the church while he and his wife took a vacation for three weeks. When they returned, an elderly couple from the church asked me to stay in their home in Haiku while they were away for 4 months. I had time to find another place to live, and I left the rented room for good.

Even during my good times and life on Maui, unresolved feelings about my mother haunted me. I finally sent her a cassette tape, telling her where I was living and what I was doing. I asked about her life. I've often wondered why I re-opened anything with her. At first, Mother's reply tapes said she was happy to hear from me and happy that I realized that I owed my mother a daughter's love. From then on, they were full-on guilt correspondences telling me how miserable she was. She claimed the neighbors hated her, and she feared they would hurt her. I also sent her some Christmas gifts that I later learned she sent to Jean because she did not want to be reminded about how I deserted her. I used to sit and listen to her rantings and argue back at the tape recorder. After I sent her the tape trying to share my religious convictions, she really went ballistic. She told my brothers and sister I was completely crazy. She also sent me a "bill" listing everything she ever spent money on me from birth on. She listed hospital costs, food and clothes and everything she could come up with. I should have returned it deducting the money I spent supporting us and the money she took when she closed our accounts. If I had not been so emotionally involved, it would have been funny.

Toward the end of working at the airport, I met a warm and funny Chinese Hawaiian man at a beach party, David Cup-Choy. He loved kids and was a lot of fun. He loved to sing and play his ukulele. He was quick to play with any kids. He laughed a lot and was happy and content with his life. Eventually, he proposed, and I accepted his engagement ring. While working a 40-hour week at Kaahumanu shopping center, I saw a lot of my fiancé as well as trained horses. In my some-what uncertain state, his simple childlike behavior was attractive. I think it was attractive because he seemed safe. I felt that someone so carefree and childlike would never hurt me. His parents were thrilled that he had a fiancé. They treated me like someone so special. Violet, David's mother was full Hawaiian, and David senior was full Chinese. Even the different culture along with moonlit walks on the beach and romantic Hawaiian songs were all so intoxicating for me.

My sister Jean came to visit at that time, and I drove her around the island. My friends, the Kaiamas helped show her places and things when I was at work. My life was full, and I was happy on my beautiful Island. I felt genuine peace and connection during that time.

With the help of Kaiamas, I found an attic apartment way up in Kula, high on the mountain of Haleakala. The apartment had an outside entrance and was self-contained. My rent consisted of being their maid which I felt I could do along with my security job. With a big house, the job was larger than I first thought, but I managed OK.

Meanwhile things with my fiancé were not good. I began to realize that I had made a big mistake. He was immature for a 38-year-old man. I watched how David's father mistreated his sweet wife and saw some of the same behaviors in David. He told me that when we were married, I would have to give up horses. Excuse me? He wanted me more stylish with makeup and nice clothes and shoes. How would I stomp on intrusive toes? He got upset anytime he saw me talking with a man and ordered me to stop talking to them.

One afternoon I phoned David to share my feelings.

"Are you breaking up with me," he asked, before I'd said more than hello.

"Yes," I answered as directly. "David, I'm not the woman you need."

"I understand," he said calmly. Did I hear a hit of relief? Maybe he'd realized our incompatibility as well.

"Come over so we can figure this out," he said.

"Ok," I said. "I do want to be friends. I care for you very much."

"You know, I do too," he said.

"Yes, well, I'll come over to return the ring."

David and I met amicably, respecting each other's feelings. There wasn't much to be said, or so I thought.

While David was quiet, his dad went ballistic. "You no good *haole,*" he screamed. Nothing I said made him back off, so I headed to the door. He refused to allow me out of his house. His wife finally phoned Reverend Bromerly at Po'okela Church. My pastor came in and convinced the man to let me go. Little did I know that this would not be the first time I was held against my will for not doing what a "man in charge" wanted me to do.

The next morning, I started a new job as the manager of Burns Security, the company providing security for the shopping mall. They also provided security throughout the island at hotels, construction sites and shopping centers. What a huge change from walking a large shopping mall to managing many guards and clients throughout all of Maui.

Meanwhile, I found the housekeeper job too much with a demanding boss. I left and took a room in town. I lived there for three whole days. The landlords were big time drug dealers. 1970s, drugs, Hawaii – go figure.

The Kaiamas found another place right on the ocean in Paia, and I moved there. The beach house didn't last long because the owner decided to sell and move back to the mainland, the US. Then, I found a house further down the shoreline where I stayed for about six months before the landlords changed their plans. That lead to another six-month arrangement. With each move, I owned a bit more, requiring a larger vehicle, and I realized that housing in Maui is tough.

The manager's job with Burns Security was taxing. I was responsible for many employees, and if a guard did not show up for work, I had to find a replacement or stand the post myself. That sometimes included overnight posts at construction sites. The owner of another security company came to me with a job offer that paid better with less responsibility. I worked the swing shift – 3 p.m. to 11 p.m. with Sundays off. I was free for church and could do other things before heading to work. Unfortunately, I worked at Whaler's Village Mall in Kaanapali. It was clear around the mountain, about an hour's drive from Paia where I lived.

Normally boring, one late evening, I was checking shop doors when I was grabbed from behind with a knife at my throat.

"You told my girlfriend not to see me."

"We're none of your business."

"Who do you think you are?" a male voice ranted.

I recognized him, an unstable man who roamed around the village. I had told a silly girl at a shoe shop to be careful.

"Why did you tell her I'm crazy?"

"I've seen you arguing with a tree," I answered, perhaps unwisely.

"Not true."

"Many times," I countered. "I've seen you talk to junk."

"You don't know anything," he said. "I'm undercover -- narcotics. I'm only pretending to be crazy."

The man was obviously deranged, and I was terrified.

"Then you must be a great actor," I improvised. "I really believed you."

"Yeah," he said more quietly, still holding the knife.

"Yes, absolutely. Don't be mad at me; you just did such a good job."

Somehow the logic reached his brain, and he did a complete change. He softened and tried to kiss me, tried to hold me.

"Maybe you can wait until I'm off duty," I stalled. "If I'm caught, I'll lose my job." I prayed he'd back off. I was still scared as he had the knife, swinging from one mood to another.

"Sure, sure, ok," he said, letting me go.

"Fine, I have to go make my rounds," I said, moving casually until out of sight.

I bolted for the security office and phoned the police who came right away, seemingly put out. They grumbled about worthless rent-a-cops. They admitted knowing the attacker but said they couldn't do anything since he didn't harm me.

Then they left. I will never understand why a person must be murdered or violently attacked before anything will be done by the authorities.

Chapter 7

Finding Myself in Service

Empty mall, one guard, stalker on the loose.

I phoned my boss.

"I'm quitting," I told him, breaking down crying. "I can't handle this job."

"It's ok, Carol. What happened?"

"Some crazy man tried to kill me with a giant knife, now he's waiting to go out on a date." The miracle is my boss didn't fire me for lunacy.

"Start at the beginning," he said.

I explained, catching my breath, stifling tears. "And, the police don't care."

"You're fine. You did fine. Leave early, alright? We can decide in the morning if you still want to quit."

The next morning, I apologized for being so soft and crying.

"Don't sweat it," he said laughing. "True, I don't get calls with guards crying, but you're the first lady I've ever had on post. And, brave. The men would've been as scared but would have hid out."

I was never again comfortable with the job at Whaler's Village. I found my nerves tense during the later hours in remote areas. Fortunately, I was too busy to dwell on the unease.

While working at Whaler's Village, I met Peggy and Stark Wolcoff who raised Arabian horses in Olinda, just southeast of Makawao. I took a job there cleaning stalls and grooming horses from 8 a.m. to 1 p.m. I then drove to the other side of the Island to work from 3 p.m. to 11 p.m. I would return home around 12:30 or 1 a.m. to then get up by 7 a.m. to drive to the Arabian stables.

I managed to do these two jobs for the next 17 months! Though young and healthy, I was exhausted. I ate most meals at MacDonald's, eating in the car while driving.

During that time, I saved my money. When I had a small reserve, I asked the Wolcoffs if I could run a riding school in the afternoons. They agreed. I earned the rental fee of the space by caring for their horses in the mornings, rather than being paid out right.

I happily gave notice at the Whaler's Village and started my school at the Olinda Arabians.

With money I had saved, I bought three saddles and equipment as well as three school horses. I leased some fields near the farm and built a shelter from timber and roofing I found in the town dump. Once people learned I had a place to teach, I built a student base quite quickly.

For the first time in quite a long time, I had a bit of free time for a social life. I learned to square dance back in grade school and in Maui there was a wonderful and friendly group who welcomed me. David and Ruth Fullaway and their three teenage girls were big time square dancers. They became close friends. To this day, they give me a $1000 a year for my youth programs. They were a special part of my Maui life, and I'm still close to them.

I enjoyed the beach and the Island. I would head for whatever beach had reasonably good waves for body surfing. If there were no waves, I would go snorkeling around the colored fish and corals. I hated lying on the beach and frying but welcomed the sun, warming up and striking up conversations with interesting people (oh my, I am missing the ocean). I met some nice people over the next year and a half. My life was filled with adventures, friends and fun. And with teaching.

Who can complain about being a trainer to the stars? Well before she was Tom Hanks' wife on *Apollo 13*, Kathleen Quinlan needed to learn to ride for an upcoming movie. She came to my school in torn jeans before that was a style and a grubby t-shirt. Stark was a total snob. On seeing Kathleen, he treated her rudely.

"Could you please be more polite?" I asked quietly, during a lesson, stepping to the edge of the arena.

"My land, my choice who comes on it," he said.

"Sure, but your comments aren't good for keeping students."

"This place doesn't need dirty hippies hanging around."

"This hippie is a movie star, Kathleen Quinlan, ever heard of her?" I said through a forced smile, waving to Kathleen.

"Anyone can claim to be some starlet."

"Yeah? Well, our "starlet" played the lead of *I Never Promised You a Rose Garden*. Heard of her now?" I asked.

Stark had a complete and sudden change of attitude. He smiled and waved. He tried to compliment her progress, but by then Kathleen paid him no attention. He was sincere in the compliment. She was an amazing athlete. Within 10 lessons, she was ready to gallop off into the sunset for her movie. To this day, she still talks about loving to ride.

The school ran well until we had an extended rainy season, and I couldn't teach. Olinda is a wet area of Maui. After much agony, I sold the horses and gave up the stable. I could not afford the feed and proper care of the animals. With much prayer and searching my heart, I decided that I needed some skill other than horse trainer or security guard. Life is full of changes.

I went from security guard to horse trainer to paramedic. I applied for a job at the Kula Hospital nursing home for the elderly and intellectually disabled. I received on-the-job training and graduated as a paramedic, allowing me to earn a full-time salary. From a kid the teachers called retarded to an adult who could handle a crisis, finishing school bolstered my esteem. Another early training for the life that would find me a decade later.

Being a paramedic is rewarding but also heartbreaking

and hard. In training, we were told we should never become emotionally involved with the patients. Impossible. The head nurse at Kula assigned me to the retarded ward (the term used at the time) where perhaps my compassion could better help the kids instead of the dying. I was happy there, and I fell in love with many of the physically and mentally disabled young patients.

In particular, I came to care deeply for Durwin. An eighteen-year-old quadriplegic, Durwin suffered from cerebral palsy. He had been sent Kula when he was 6 months old. I strongly believed he was not retarded but just unable to communicate because of his extreme condition. I started taking him home on weekends and letting him see more of the world than the rooms he had grown up in.

Serious migraines which would incapacitate me became my next challenge. As they increased in frequency, the head nurse felt that I was not emotionally strong enough for the work. I would become furious when I saw staff abusing patients which was often.

At about the same time, I found a stable in a dry area, in Pukalani at the Wai Ulu Farm stables where I could run my school. I turned in my resignation at Kula Hospital and again began to establish my school. I bought my own horse and got a beautiful Golden Retriever puppy. Another fresh start.

I now lived in an apartment in the lower part of a house that a young woman and her elderly psychologist husband were renting. When the couple moved to another house further up the mountain, they rented me a room in a shack on the land. The shack had one room with no plumbing and a single light bulb hanging from the center of the ceiling. Though the space stayed cold and wet, with a dog, cat and horse I couldn't be choosy. Years later I would meet entire families and lost children with far less than I had in that little shack on the mountain - on other mountains, on the other side of the world. The Lord was preparing me for Uganda even though I didn't realize it at the time.

The Wai Ulu stables were successful, and I again was enjoying my life with the horses.

However, I missed Durwin terribly. When I could bring him home with me on weekends, he would cry and vomit when I drove him back on Sunday evening. My own life was not stable, and I could not think of what to do.

The young woman married to the psychologist, in whose shack I lived, was a self-mutilator who sliced her arms and legs with knives when she was upset. Great. Here we go again. One day she came raging to the stable.

"I know you're interested in my husband," she accused.

"NO WAY," I said, startled and unequivocal.

"I know you are," she persisted.

"I'm absolutely not attracted to your husband," I responded.

My tone shifted something in her mind.

"What's wrong with him?" she screamed.

She built herself into a frenzy, screaming about my

supposed impugning of her husband. She took out a knife and sliced herself deeply, bleeding profusely.

I ran into the office and called her husband who came running and drove her to the hospital. Time for another move.

Around this time, Carl Powers, who owned a pig farm in the dryer part of Olinda came to me with an offer to develop his place into a horse farm. He had been following my work at Wai Ulu Farm. Carl said he would work along with me to build the stalls and fences and make a training arena. Once finished, he planned to move to Alaska, and I would run the horse farm.

I accepted – after we drew up an agreement. I was slowly learning to be more careful about what I got involved in. Well, maybe.

This was now 1982.

I began developing my stables which we named Mauka Lani Stables – Mountain Skies in the Hawaiian language. We held a grand opening where several hundred people attended. There were twenty-five stalls and five turn out paddocks as well as a large training arena. I placed a small shack that had been used to sell sodas at the rodeos on the embankment overlooking the arena. It served as a horse show stage to keep ribbons and a place for the announcer and PA system.

At the time, I was a deacon at Po'okela Church. The church had built a new house for our pastor and family. I rented the old parsonage. After so many different houses and living situations, I was thrilled to get this old house, originally constructed in 1843. It had a beautiful view of the mountains and was completely mine. This turned out to be the last house I lived in on Maui. I loved that house and will always have wonderful memories of it.

I felt relatively stable, and after much prayer, I decided to get full time custody of Durwin, who I missed terribly. I knew he wasn't being treated as well as he deserved. How could the hospital caregivers be so callous with what I'd been denied? While in Hawaii, I had surgery for personal female problems. The procedure was more radical than expected, and I would never be able to have children. Even though I was in my late 30s, I had hoped to have at least one child. I was devastated to learn the chance had passed. I was randomly reading my Bible while recovering and came across Isaiah 54. The passage says "to rejoice barren one for you will have more children than the married." At that time, I felt it referred to all the kids I had worked with up to this point. Years later, I realized the passage was referencing many more.

Many people strongly urged me to reconsider adopting Durwin because he needed much care. I went to the hospital and asked what would be required to gain custody.

"That's not possible," the nurse in charge said with some sympathy.

"Why not?"

"He'll be too much for you, single and working, to manage."

"I have it planned out," I said, having already figured

out how to have him with me at the stables.

"In all likelihood, he only has a year or so to live," she said.

"Then let them be good years," I said, purposefully using the plural.

"If you insist," she conceded, "we'll contact Durwin's parents."

His parents objected. They did not wish the community to learn they had a handicapped son. I went to legal aid and was given a wonderful, caring lawyer. He talked with the parents, pointing out that we would do everything possible to get custody. If they fought adoption, the newspapers would take an interest, revealing their secret. They signed the papers. I became Durwin's legal guardian in 1984 with full custody and government assistance for his medical needs and care.

Durwin was so full of love, and I was overjoyed to have him in my life. At the riding school, I built a platform with a mattress in the announcing shack, providing a good view of the arena. I also installed a TV in the upper corner for him to watch on slow days. He became a part of life at the stable and even at the horse shows. The kids loved pushing him everywhere in the wheelchair, and he really loved riding horses. He also loved swimming in the ocean and going shopping in town and seeing so many new things. I was amazed to watch him as he saw new things. He was totally fascinated when he saw his first fire. He enriched my life in more ways than I knew were possible.

Many people who at first were a bit scared of

someone so different learned to love him dearly. He taught us how someone who may seem a bit different still has much to offer.

The stable and students grew and were known and successful throughout the island. I put on horse shows and attended many. I brought a few hopeless horses along to be champions. I also had many lost, little rich kids who depended on me for a lot more than learning to ride. One 13-year-old girl was even abandoned with me for a year. Another teen came to the school all legs and elbows. She rode an ugly little Appaloosa and cringed when her mom grew upset when she placed poorly in horse shows. I knew she had talent. I put her to work helping train my young horses. Lehua Custer is now a Grand Prix dressage champion with her own school in Los Angeles.

Mauka Lani became the biggest stable on Maui. We fit well with the famous Maui Horse Center. The matron there now accepted me as an accomplished trainer and welcomed my students to learn from world famous trainers.

I think my years training in Hawaii were my own best learning years. I learned to smile, and I learned to weep.

Chapter 8

Heartbreak

Growing in strength with the Lord, I happily participated with the Po'okela Church in Makawao. Reverend Vernon Tom, the pastor at the time, with his wife and two boys became like family to me. Through some serious counseling, Vern helped me let go of my past in many ways. In prayers and counseling, I forgave myself for many things that I did not feel good about in the past.

I still held hatred I had not faced. At this stage, I wanted more than anything for Mother to experience the joy of knowing God. I felt she could become a happy person if she would only turn her anger away and accept Jesus. I made a cassette tape where I shared my faith and desire for her to have the same. I apologized for any pain I caused her. I forgave her. I emphasized that if she would turn to Jesus, she could finally have peace in her heart. I asked Pastor Vern to listen to the tape to be sure I said nothing that might be taken wrongly. In my heart, I had completely forgiven her. Pastor Vern gave it back with tears in his eyes and said that I must send it.

Unfortunately, the tape was not received with love but instead with huge anger. I never again heard a word from my mother. Instead, in her anger, she told my sister Jean that I had become a religious freak, claiming I said all sorts of terrible things to her. She vented to my two brothers with the same anger. Jean was indignant and defended me which angered Mother and led her to stop corresponding with Jean as well. Mother died a bitter and angry old lady in November of 1988.

Life on Maui encompassed friendships, horse training and shows, and students. The one negative aspect in my life was ongoing migraines that plagued me terribly. I would get one or two debilitating migraines in a month. Often my friends would drive me to the hospital where they gave me a strong pain medicine by injections. I even traveled to a specialized pain management and headache clinic advertised in Washington State and spent a week there. Nothing seemed to help. When hit with one, I couldn't function.

Durwin also had health issues and was hospitalized several times. He had trouble swallowing food. Enough went into his lungs causing pneumonia several times. He finally had to be flown to Oahu and have a tube inserted directly into his stomach. With the successful surgery, his health returned quite well. At first, he cried bitterly, wanting to eat food. He had a hard time understanding why I no longer fed him. Instead, he received a liquid meal every four hours, 24 hours a day. He slept through the night feedings, and I became so exhausted that I fell right back to sleep myself.

In April of 1992, I was fixing a fence up on a hill in heavy undergrowth late in the evening after everyone had gone home. Seeing some ripe bananas, I picked one for me and another for Whoopie, a horse in the pasture. I did not hear Whoopie at a gallop coming down the steep hill. I remember turning in time to see her on top of me and then blackness. A woman filling her pickup truck with manure for her garden saw Whoopie looking at something on the ground as she was driving away. She turned back, sure she would worry if she kept driving away. She came up the hill, saw me unconscious and bleeding. She grabbed Whoopie with a belt around her neck, dragged her down to a stall and ran shouting for someone to phone for an ambulance. She then hurried back and rolled me on my side so I would not choke on my blood.

I was partially gaining consciousness as paramedics strapped me on a stretcher. I kept mumbling about Durwin. The driver was a dear friend who phoned his wife to get Durwin and take care of him. In the emergency room, things were strange. I remember no pain at all. Without words, I was communicating with my late father. I felt a clear knowledge that Dad understood things that happened many years ago that I still carried guilt about. Suddenly, I was again present in the room but as an unemotional observer. The doctors were concerned about my head injury, and one kept saying he did not think I would make it. I have learned that our loved ones are close when we ourselves are close to death.

Another decided to sew my face injuries to prevent serious scarring. When he started sewing my face, I immediately went from no pain to indescribable, horrendous pain. I was put into an MRI tube, very hard because I felt as if I would throw up. Finally, once I was sent to a room, I was given as much pain control as they dared with my head injury. I had surgery to replace my jaw with a titanium jaw a day or two later. My jaw was wired shut so I could only take liquids for three months.

I also had a broken left ankle that medical personnel forgot for several days. They told me to try walking a little, and I asked, "What about my broken leg?" That sure did cause a commotion when they realized what they forgot. They belatedly put a cast on my leg. I slowly healed and was released from the hospital after 10 days.

In another few days, I started teaching again while sitting in Durwin's room. With my jaw wired, I had difficulty speaking clearly. I struggled teaching while just sitting because I used to be quite active when teaching. Thankfully, many of the "barn rats," teens who basically lived at the stable, helped with tacking up the horses and spotting for beginners while I sat in the booth overlooking the arena, instructing over a loudspeaker. I'm so grateful to those young boys who helped me keep things going while I was healing.

Only a few months later, I was working with a young

horse who stumbled with me. She somersaulted, and I flew over her head and landed on my back on a log. Though terribly painful, I waited four days to see a doctor. I had broken the T12 in my back and was put in a large body support. I slept in a chair because I could not lie down. I struggled through one problem after another, but being a stubborn person, I fought through and continued teaching and caring for Durwin.

Tragedy struck on August 5, 1993. The day had been busy with many lessons, a veterinarian for a sick horse visiting along with the horseshoer to reset several sets of shoes on the animals. I fed Durwin his 2 p.m. feeding, saw his diaper was dry, so I left him with the TV. I noticed the mattress pulled a bit from the far wall, and I thought to myself that I should push it back against the wall the next time I came to check on him.

I was on the other side of the barn when I heard a friend screaming for someone to come fast. I raced through the barn, thinking a kid had been thrown from a horse. The woman was with Durwin. He had gotten wedged between the wall and the mattress.

"Phone 9-1-1, call an ambulance," I yelled, starting CPR immediately. I continued with CPR until the ambulance arrived.

"Carol, I'm here, let me take over," the paramedic said when he arrived.

I was frantic, struggling to stay at Durwin's side.

"Do you want me to do everything possible?" he asked, as he and his partner moved me from the room. He must have known Durwin was beyond aid, but he was a good friend.

"Yes, everything, save him," I said as I sank down outside, almost passing out from the CPR and fear.

After some time, the ambulance attendants came out.

"It's no use," my friend said. "Durwin is gone."

The rest of the afternoon is a blur. The police came for the report and the coroner came to take Durwin away. My pastor came and prayed but everything was unreal. Several people wanted me to come home with them, but I wanted to be alone.

Durwin's parents came that evening – they never visited him when he was alive – and asked me why I let him get in trouble. Conscious that Durbin suffocated because of the mattress I should have fixed, I did not need them telling me anything. They finally left. I walked the roads most of the night. I wanted to scream but could not.

The next days were painfully difficult with the funeral scheduled for Sunday after church service. The church filled to overflowing. The parents sat up front as family which I found so grim. Somehow during the service, I forgave them, realizing the loss was harder for them than for me. The mother especially realized that she was never a mom to him.

I turned to working double time at the stable. I gave lessons and fixed broken fences and everything else I could do to stifle the hurt. One evening about ten days later, a young girl who lived in a cottage with her mom on the grounds called me to the stable. The girl's dog had badly injured one of my cats, and the intestines were exposed. The cat was in much pain. I phoned the vet to please put it out of its misery.

When I got back home, I started shaking and crying and could not stop. I phoned a good friend, and she came to my house and spent the night with me. She encouraged me to cry and talk. The next day, I phoned the stable and announced I was taking two weeks off. I spent my time in prayer and walking alone. My friends and church were wonderful. I gradually returned to the full swing of life, slowly healing. What felt impossible weeks ago, was slowly starting to take form. Healing from heartbreak. I also took a two-week vacation with my friend Patty. We drove around Western Canada and Washington State. That was the best vacation that I have ever had.

I came back refreshed and continued with the training and teaching. But I had lost my courage. I no longer trained the wilder horses, and I avoided jumping. Once courage is lost as a horse trainer, it is hard to continue. I was changed by trauma. However, I did enjoy dressage and was doing basic training level and some first level with several horses. I thought that I had found my way back again.

Then, in 1995, my life took a completely different direction.

Chapter 9

Uncertainty and Intuition

C ompetitive horse shows – another task.
New horses, new saddles, riding clothes
- unimportant.

Early in the spring of 1995, I felt I should be contributing more to the world. To this dissatisfaction, I argued silently: "I run a successful stable, more so than any before. I am active at church. I have many friends and enjoy more time with them than in the past. Maui is my home, where I belong." I have since learned to listen to my intuition rather than try to talk myself out of its guidance, no matter how crazy it sounds at the time.

I increased my work with troubled children sent by the local government for horse riding therapy. I continued working with handicapped riding therapy groups. Neither filled the empty space.

On August 30th, I listened to the sermon, the story of

Abraham. God asked Abraham to sacrifice his favored son, Isaac. Abraham bound Isaac to an altar and would have given his child to God, a story of profound faith and obedience.

I silently prayed that if the Lord wanted me, I was there for Him.

WOW!!! What a powerful answer I received.

Children in Africa needed me.

I did not hear a voice or see a vision. I just knew I was needed. The knowledge was so real that I had tears running down my face and a joy I cannot put into words. I left the service with huge excitement.

"Michael," I called out to Pastor Vern's son, the first person I could corner. "I'm going to Africa."

"Really?" he said, as if I were planning an extravagant vacation. "That's neat!"

"God told me I'm needed in Africa," I said breathlessly.

I'm not sure what he saw in me. He took me seriously right away, maybe because we had known each other since he was a kid.

"That's wonderful," he said with sincerity.

"I can't believe it. I've been fretting that I'm not doing enough. I told God, and He gave me a mission."

"I'm happy for you, Carol. I hope you can make it work," he said.

Pastor Vern finished greeting people and shaking hands, so I rushed to tell him.

"You know I'm always available for you," he said, looking at me with a worried expression.

"I know you are," I said, oblivious to the real meaning of his comment. "I can't wait to get going."

"If you're having any problems or need to talk with someone…," I realized he wasn't as receptive as Michael.

Others who heard my news had the same worrisome reaction, yet my excitement held.

I went to the stable owners the same afternoon and told them I was giving them a two month notice to find another person to run the stable. The next day, I went to the library between training lessons and took out books on Africa. First Hawaii, now Africa. Libraries then, and Google now.

The Kahului Christian bookstore loaned me a book listing many different missions and information about them. I spent my evenings filling out forms from the different missionary agencies. I was quite startled to learn that most agencies require the missionary to obtain a promise of a monthly allotment paid to the organization. In turn, the agency covers the missionary with health insurance, travel costs, rentals and other needs. They required more than I made in a month at the stable!

The only replies I received were negative. I did not have enough Bible training. At 51, I was too old. Horse training was not needed in Africa. I only had a high school education. Just as well, I relented as I couldn't see myself begging my family and friends for support.

I continued my work at the stable but told my students I was planning on leaving and why. At the end of September, the stable had a huge good-bye party for me with much emotion and love. I left my dog Cleo with the stable where she was welcomed although I missed her terribly. A female police officer took my horse, and a woman on the other side of the island took my cat Gigi. She was 10 years old and followed me like a dog and rode around on my shoulders. Giving up my animals was incredibly difficult.

I worried about how I would get to Africa but still knew I'd get there. I sold much of my equipment and gave away a lot. I sold my horse trailer, leaving only my car which I needed to get around on the island. I worried about living without any income, so I applied and was immediately hired at a home for severely retarded adults. I was accepted with the understanding I might leave with little notice once I knew how I was going to Africa, even though I knew nothing of the continent and had never traveled except within the US.

By November, my house stood almost empty. With no animals, I felt a bit foolish and lost. One Saturday evening, I prayed, asking God how I was to get myself where He had called. I suddenly realized that I was depending on my own means and not enough on His. The next day, a group from Haggai Institute attended church with two Africans in attendance. Haggai is an evangelistic training program for people from developing countries. After church, I introduced myself to the Africans and shared my calling with them. I spent the day driving them around the island. They were interested in having me come to help in their countries. One was from Nigeria and one from Ghana.

I arrived home that evening and found a message on my answering machine from a friend who had met a Christian singing group, Limit X, on Oahu and told them about me. She said they were excited to meet me so that I might help run an orphanage they had in Luwero, Uganda. The next day, I flew to Oahu and met with the young Ugandan men, Denis Sempebwa, Isaac Ruccebigango and Paul Mutebi. Paul's father had the orphanage.

I knew I should go to Uganda. The others who I had met were vague about why they needed me. Even though I was completely naive about the habit of Africans seeing Americans as walking money, I sensed that in them. On the other hand, the Limit X group seemed much more focused.

I arrived back on Maui at the next day, the end of November. I resigned from my job and finished preparations to leave for Uganda. I had already applied for and received a passport. I finished paying a few debts, set up a power of attorney with a friend to help with banking – she is still helping – and gave away anything I wouldn't be carrying with me. I sold my car with the buyer agreeing that I could drive it until I left. Once again, I was shedding all my physical possessions in pursuit of my peace.

People now took me seriously. Friends planned good-bye parties, many filled with tears. Reality finally hit me. The Sunday before Christmas, the church had a commissioning service for me, gave me many leis and surrounded me with prayers. I spent the next week visiting friends and packing suitcases of any possessions such as pictures and some things I could not carry but found too hard to let go. These I asked friends to keep for me. Christmas Eve service was emotional, and I was asked to speak. Christmas day seemed lonely and long. I shared dinner with friends, but my mind was travelling already. Was I ready? Would I make a difference? Was the separation from friends and comfort worth venturing into the unknown? Leaning into uncertainty is terrifying, and I thought of every reason imaginable that I was not the right person for the job. On Christmas day evening, a big thunderstorm hit, unusual for Maui. I welcomed the storm as a gift and a good omen as I love thunderstorms.

I am often reminded that God freed Abraham of the demand for Isaac, his son, and rewarded him, Genesis 22:17:

"I will surely bless you and make your descendants as numerous as the stars in the sky and as the sand on the seashore. Your descendants will take possession of the cities of their enemies, and through your offspring all nations on earth will be blessed."

My early doubts have long passed. I am blessed everyday by the fortitude of every child I serve, by the stars in their bright eyes and minds as they take their place in the world, sometimes on distant shores where they thrive and serve others.

Chapter 10

Hoale To Mzungu

Many friends came to the airport to see me off. I never knew saying good-bye could be so hard. I will always remember walking down the airplane tunnel and turning around to wave for the last time. Once in the air, I felt scared and excited at the same time.

I stopped in California to stay with a friend, Donna Fleming, before meeting Limit X on New Year's Day. I celebrated New Year's Eve with Donna in her apartment. I felt ill but chose to ignore it. On New Year's Day, I took a bus in the pouring rain to a train that would take me to the airport. The bus trip was overwhelming as I felt ill and had all my luggage. Little did I know this was the relaxed part. I was supposed to meet the Limit X boys at the airport and grew nervous when I did not find them. They finally arrived, and a large group of us began the first leg of our journey to Uganda.

We spent a night in an airport hotel in Gatwick, England, where my illness turned to a high fever and cough. The group which included an American couple as well as an American young woman engaged to the lead of Limit X went out for the evening. I stayed in bed and took some flu medicine, hoping it would help. The next morning, we boarded for the final trip to Entebbe, Uganda. I was so, so sick by then!

I sat next to an angry Kenyan man who grumbled and complained about everything. I also saw a lady with a jacket that said African Inland Missions, one of the organizations I had applied to. I went to introduce myself.

"Hi, I'm Carol Adams," I said, extending my hand. "I'm also going to work in Uganda."

"Hello," she said, "what agency are you with?"

"I'm not with an agency. I'm traveling with Limit X, the Christian music group. They've asked me to help with an orphanage."

She sniffed, ignoring my hand, maybe because she could tell I was sick, I thought.

"You should go home," she said.

"Too late for that," I said. "I'm committed."

"Well, you have no right coming to Uganda without being sponsored by an agency."

"I tried that, didn't work. I believe God has shown me an alternative path."

"You've no idea what you're doing," she answered rudely. "People like you are a problem in my country."

"Her country?" I thought, leaving this white,

American woman to her opinion. Alas, this was the first of many such reactions.

We finally arrived at the Entebbe International Airport twenty-five miles outside of Kampala after a very, very long flight. The Limit X group were met by a throng of relatives and fans. Several vehicles called *matatus,* 14-seater minibuses, waited for us once we cleared our luggage. In the crowd and terrible heat, everything felt strange and a bit scary. I took a window seat for the trip to the Sheraton Hotel in Kampala.

The Republic of Uganda is a landlocked country in East-Central Africa. It sits in the middle of South Sudan, Ethiopia, Kenya, Tanzania and the Democratic Republic of the Congo. Boundaries include the Rwenzori Mountains to the west and Lake Victoria (the source of the Nile) along the south. The equator runs through the southern part of Uganda, south of Kampala, the capital. While English and Swahili are the official languages, there are over 40 languages spoken within Uganda's borders.

I arrived on a hot day, and the huge numbers of people everywhere struck me right away. The population in Uganda stood at about 20 million (now it's double, in part due to refugees). Over 80% of Ugandans lived then and now in rural areas. That still left a million residing in Kampala at the time. Now the Kampala population stands at over 1.6 million.

There were so many people walking or on bicycles and small motorcycles called *bodas,* many serving as taxis. Crazy drivers on the *bodas* wove in and out of traffic, driving anywhere, in either direction, bouncing over center road barriers and sidewalks, where there happened to be such. Here, everyone is on their own once they get behind a wheel. If you are not an aggressive driver, you are in trouble. Horns blow constantly. There seem to be no traffic rules. The middle of the city is modern like any city in the world, but once you get a bit off the center streets, there are open sewers, potholes large enough to sink a car wheel, deep ditches along the sides of the roads, and even cows, goats and chickens running free. Groups of kids kick balls made from tightly wrapped and tied plastic bags with people in the streets weaving in and out of cars, trucks, busses and bodas. The air quality is horrible with no emission laws and huge trucks and busses putting out black exhaust. The noise level of horns, people hawking all types of goods, matatu conductors yelling different destinations and construction seems never to slow down.

Tens of thousands of people ran to the city from the countryside looking for a better life and instead created slums. Walking in Kampala is like walking in a National Geographic scene. The photos, however, do not carry the smells or the noise and even the fears. If you get caught in a traffic jam, hawkers appear at your windows selling anything from watches to chickens to fruits and almost anything else. Beggars come to your windows and street kids holding filthy babies. Hundreds of dirty ragged kids look out from garbage and rubbish everywhere.

People live in shops made from old materials with

rocks holding the roofs down. They sell all sorts of things including meat hung by the legs in doorways covered with flies. At first, it was a surprise, but now I'm amused by the signs that hang everywhere, over doors, market walls, etc. The day I arrived; one sign stayed in my mind – "Pop in for your coffin."

We finally reached the hotel, which was a bit rough by US standards, and expensive, which worried me somewhat.

Limit X were immediately busy with setting up for a concert which we went to at the Kampala Pentecostal Church. I still had a bad flu but greatly enjoyed the concert. The group had many activities planned, including a trip to Jinja on the shores of Lake Victoria and the start of the Nile River. During this hectic time, my eyes filled with sights as my nose took in smells of burnt rubber and open-air abattoirs, exhaust and heavy perfumes, open sewers and garbage all over.

On the last day the boys were in Uganda, they went to Luwero to see the orphanage and introduce me. The orphanage was dilapidated – at least by my then still American vision. I was shocked to find a rundown building with no orphans and squatters who had moved into the house. Paul's father saw my white skin and told me that if I wished to open an orphanage on his land I had to pay him $1500 dollars a month. I did not begin to have that kind of money. The boys were upset to find such a situation but had no idea what to do. They were sorry and suggested I should go back home.

NO WAY!!!!!! was I giving up that easily. So, I

accompanied the boys to the airport and said goodbye.

Rose Musoke, one of the Limit X organizers, offered to take me to the Namarembe Guest House while I tried to figure out what my next steps should be. I gladly took that offer because the Sheraton was fast eating up my money. Late that night, after getting settled and Rose drove away, it hit me – I was alone and had no idea what next!

With the power out that night, I just collapsed in the bed of the small, hot room. I still suffered from the flu I caught in California. I woke in the morning and timidly stepped out of my room. At the guest house, both men and women shared the bathroom and toilets. I had to explore a bit for breakfast. I felt lost and scared (a recurring theme over the next several years) and spent time sitting around writing letters to my friends back on Maui. People often say how brave I was. I was NOT brave, I was terrified.

The second day, I ventured into the city. Clueless on how to catch a taxi, I headed out walking and asking directions.

The city was crowded, dirty, hot, and smelly. I saw terribly maimed beggars everywhere. Crossing roads was crazy. I got run down by a bicycle at one crossing because I looked left instead of right. As I brushed off my scrapes, the angry bike man kept yelling "stupid *mzungu*!" I don't blame him. Driving is on the left side here. Also, I learned that I was a *mzungu* – white person. I left Maui as a *haole* and now became a *mzungu*. Life is funny.

Tired from walking, overwhelmed by the sights, getting sicker by the minute, I needed to get back to the guest house. Lost, I started walking in the direction I thought it should be. I was in a commercial area filled with shops and people and *bodas* and beggars when suddenly I heard gunshots. They were quite close. The streets emptied immediately while I stood there like a dummy. A man grabbed my arm and yelled "*mzungu*, come" and dragged me into a small shop. There everyone was talking in their own language and peeking out the door. After some time, they slowly ventured out.

I asked an English-speaking man for directions. He pointed out a large tower visible from many places and said to always go that way and I would make it. After walking about half a mile, I passed near a large brick wall when I smelled a terrible stink. What I first thought was a pile of rags was actually a lady who had been dead for some time. I almost got sick. I hurried past and arrived at the guest house quite shook up. I recorded my venture on my small tape recorder.

The days went by with no idea what my next step should be. I thank God for Rose Musoke who visited me several times. She drove me to a doctor who diagnosed me with pneumonia. He told me to stay quiet, take the medicine he prescribed, and drink a lot of fluids. Rose helped me open a bank account as keeping much cash in Uganda is NOT a good idea. She showed me how to catch the loaded *matatus* which served as taxis. They function sort of like a carpool that you catch by going to stands where the minibuses congregate. They are usually white with blue blocks. Painted slogans adorn windscreens and back windows. "Try Jesus." "Better be late than never." "Insha Allah." "Tsunami." "God is great." "Prosperity for All." "Hosana!"

As the days dragged by, I met other residents at the guest house, many of them missionaries. All the white people told me to go home, that I had no right to come to the country on a whim. The Ugandan people were different, though. They encouraged me and prayed with me and gave me hope that some answers would come.

On my tenth day at the guest house, Rose invited me to a Bible study in Mukono where an old missionary American couple, Grover and Helena Willcox, lived. They prayed with me when I shared my situation and my weakening faith. The next day, I received a call from Simeon Wiehler who ran the Besiniya Boy's orphanage in Mukono. The Wilcox's' attended the same church as Simeon and told him about me. Simeon offered to pick me up and house me there until I knew where I should be. What a wonderful relief! Simeon arrived the next morning in an old pickup truck and threw my luggage in the back. We then ran several errands around the city, including a stop where he introduced me to Sam Mutabazi, a member on Simeon's orphanage board. Finally heading towards the orphanage, I cannot express how relieved I felt even though Simeon made it plain that there was no work for me. A spiritual man, he was certain that God had a plan for me.

When we arrived at the orphanage up on a hill, many boys came running, excited to have a visitor. The home consisted of about six round huts with six to ten boys living in each and a large building up a long stone staircase with a kitchen and large combination dining/study area with long picnic-type tables. The matron lived in a double circle house with her husband and one little girl. They lived in rooms at one end of the building and on the other end there were six beds where some of the girls who helped wash and cook lived. They put me with the girls. The matron was not happy at all to have me there while the husband stayed quiet. Simeon had his own little cottage located high on a hill. The air was clear and fresh with the sweet scent of trees and different plants. No more noise of the city but rather kids laughing and playing and birds of every description. Such a HUGE relief!

After supper and sitting around with the boys for a while, I headed to bed, tired and still quite sick. I was so grateful for the sagging, uncomfortable bed. The girls sat around talking in their own language, shy. Once things grew quiet and lights were out for some time, the door to the room opened. The matron came sneaking in and started looking through my luggage. At first, I pretended to sleep but finally started moving around when she kept handling everything. She hurried out, but her rifling showed me that my initial feeling about her was correct. I was slowly getting better at listening to my intuition.

The next few days passed and my breathing slowly improved. The boys were great fun to talk to. When he had time, Simeon showed me quite a bit about Uganda.

He took me on a tour of the trading center in Mukono. A trading center is a large open market selling goods and food, some cooked over small charcoal stoves. He introduced me as his jjaja which means grandmother. Many years later I traveled to Rwanda as an honored guest at his wedding.

My days at the Besiniya orphanage was a time of great joy for me. I was in a safe place while trying to figure out my next steps. These were exciting days, getting to know the teen boys, adjusting to fresh foods, animal sounds, pungent smells, vibrant colors and the flow of a rowdy day. The kids were filled with joy, fun loving and accepting of this "old lady" who was with them. I learned that young people are taught to always kneel when greeting older people. At first it bothered me, but Simeon explained that the culture insisted on good manners from their young people. I cannot say that I was not scared, but at the same time I was filled with excitement and hope and wonder at the new world I found myself in. I was in regular prayer and was given strength and given people who came into my life when I needed them most. I never doubted that God was behind all of this.

After a couple of days, a good looking, young African man came to the home. He had spent his teen years there. Recently graduated from Mukono University, he had studied to be an Anglican priest. Reverend Sam. His spirituality impressed me as did his desire to help disadvantaged people and orphans. He was from a village in west Uganda called Fort Portal. After talking for several days off and on, he asked me to join him back in his home village. He planned to start an NGO (non-government organization). Little things bothered me about him such as the way he would leave me carrying heavy packages up the hill to the home with my still difficult breathing while he strode ahead. We took several trips into the city and again he would take off leaving me to fend for myself. I found the lack of any public toilets the hardest to manage. In those days, *mzungu*-type fast food places with toilets in the building didn't exist. He completely lacked Western manners, but I decided that must be the African way.

I had better get used to it.

Chapter 11

Darkness Before
the Storm

T he days in the city and orphanage at Mukono passed in a blur before we finally headed out on a *matatu*. The 14-seater minibus carried at least 20 people along with all sorts of luggage and babies and huge piles on the roof. The back door gaped open because of the stuff crammed in, allowing heavy exhaust fumes to enter. I was the only *mzungu* in the *matatu*. After much shouting and cramming yet one more and one more person in, we headed out to Fort Portal. By the time we arrived in Fort Portal, at dusk, I was in desperate shape to relieve my bladder – with no place to be found. Again, Rev. Sam showed no concern for my welfare when I brought it up. He instead rented a car, and we proceeded to a place called Nyakasura Secondary

School taught by a priest, Rev. Charles Ndolerere, the pastor of the school who became a friend.

Poor Rev. Charles had no idea we were coming because there were no phones back in those days. He, however, warmly welcomed us. He gave me a room of one of his extended family while she shared with another girl elsewhere. His quiet wife also welcomed us warmly and fixed tea and food. The facilities consisted of a weak latrine (of utmost importance at the time) with a cloth for a door. They had indoor plumbing but no running water. To bathe, we had to carry in water from outside, but at least could stand inside.

What a huge relief (yes!) to have the Nyakasura school to start learning about the country and the challenges faced daily. I was, however, seeing everything through Western eyes. I felt quite overwhelmed with a hugely different lifestyle to anything I had known or even imagined. I remember being amazed that the kids in the home did not own a single toy and were required to do many chores.

When I first arrived in Fort Portal, the town seemed strange to me with dirt streets, small shops and the market. The streets in town are now all paved. We have electricity and even solar streetlights. We now are known as the tourist city of Uganda! Considered a gateway to many of Uganda's natural beauties, Fort Portal lies about 5000 feet above sea level in the northern foothills of the Mountains of the Moon (the Rwenzori Mountains), the source of the Nile River. It's near the Kibale Forest, famous for its chimpanzees.

I am grateful to Rev. Charles. He took me on hikes to find stunning lakes. The steep hills south of Fort Portal secret away one of the densest collections of crater lakes in the world, some as deep as 400 meters. The serene lakes were formed 8,000-10,000 years ago by violent volcanic activity, exploding ash and rock for miles. Active while the Pyramids in Egypt were being built, today the volcanoes lie dormant. Some of the lakes have glass-clear water; others are overgrown with vegetation. Huge trees, plants and flowers of all types are everywhere. Rev. Charles' mom is an herbalist healer. Charles picked some plants and had me chew them to alleviate my still heavy cough. They cured me almost immediately, and I was breathing well for the first time since reaching Uganda. A few of the lakes still release the distinct smell of sulfur. The soothing setting is perfect for swimming (except for the lake with a grumpy lone hippo), surrounded by chittering black-white-and-red colobus monkeys and chirping, as well as screaming, tropical birds. The bird voices are amazing with some singing a four-note tune while others have raucous voices and others almost sounded like humans talking.

We hiked past villages where kids came running calling out "mzungu--how are you?" We passed banana plantations, huge gardens and waterfalls to reach the lakes. On a sunny day, we could see the Rwenzori Mountains of the Moon in the distance. I often told Rev. Charles he could be a tour guide. With Rev. Charles' help and friendliness and that of Rev. Sam's brother Churchill, a teacher at the Nyakasura School, I began feeling a tad less lonely and scared.

Rev. Sam spent a fair amount of time running here and there, getting documentation for the NGO he was forming, and he often left me sitting in a small restaurant in town.

As I think back on things, I am thankful for the slow start for the work I was called to. I would have been completely unqualified to run the orphanage in Luwero. I had too much to learn about the laws and cultures of the country. Fort Portal is filled with activity of *bodas* and bicycles and huge lorries delivering goods from the city. When I arrived, the village had less than 40,000 people, now we have nearly 55,000. At the time, mad people wandered around freely. There were hardly any *bzungu* around, so people would turn and stare at me. Kids called out, "*Mzungu*, how are you?" as those were some of the first English words they learned. M*zungu* is singular and *bzungu* is plural in Rutooro, a dialect of Bantu, one of Uganda's four distinct language families.

We quickly realized we needed a car of some sort to travel around Fort Portal. On a visit back to Kampala, Simeon helped us find a small pickup truck for six million Ugandan Shillings, at that time about $4000 US. Out of my reach while I struggled to get my personal funds transferred to Uganda.

Rev. Sam brought me to meet a man named John Katuramu. He lived in a six-story, fancy building called the Uganda House that he owned, along with an airplane and the Voice of Tooro -- VOT, the first radio station in Western Uganda. I am sure that he owns a lot more. His son runs the VOT and other businesses. Businesses occupied the lower floors of Uganda House while Katuramu lived in the penthouse. Security cameras and armed guards followed us as we moved through the building.

Katuramu was the regent for the 4-year old child king of Tooro Kingdom, one of the five traditional kingdoms of Uganda, whose father had recently died. I had heard rumors that he had murdered the king with poison but didn't believe it. Later he was convicted for murdering the Tooro Kingdom prince who was trying to prove that Katuramu murdered the king – his brother. As regent, Katuramu received a title and the huge sum of money that went with the regency. He hired a hitman to kill the prince, foolishly using a written contract. The prince was assassinated in a small pub next to the library right here in Fort Portal. Several *boda* men caught the killer who had the contract in his pocket. Katuramu has been asking forgiveness and seeking release, but thank God, so far, no luck. His continued incarceration is amazing as he has enough money to bribe judges and officials.

Katuramu agreed to loan us the 6,000,000 shillings with a promise of a quick repayment – one month. I knew my funds would arrive from the States, so I bought the truck and put it in the name of High Hope NGO.

We couldn't stay very long with Rev. Charles and family as they were packed in already. I found us a large, old, formerly British home owned by the Anglican

Diocese near the Canon Apolo teaching school and close to Rev. Charles, about 7 kilometers outside of Fort Portal. It was on a large compound (lawn) with fragrant eucalyptus trees. The large older house had electricity, sporadic, and indoor plumbing after a fashion. The water did not run most of the time. I had no furniture, so I slept on a mattress on the floor of one of the bedrooms. I had no refrigerator and stove. I tried to cook with a small kerosene burning stove and sometimes used charcoal outside. I knew nothing about cooking, especially without packaged foods. I was a completely spoiled American used to fast foods or frozen dinners.

Rev. Sam did not seem happy with my lack of skills. He became difficult to live with. He expected me to act like his slave, cooking and cleaning and all. He had a scary temper and was terribly moody, sometimes flying into a rage. I was in frequent prayer, asking the Lord what I should do.

He refused any jobs offered by the Bishop. As a new deacon, he was supposed to work in a church to gain experience, but he wanted his freedom. He was applying to go to a university in the US, and I prayed that would happen. I planned to stay in Fort Portal and manage the NGO.

Nothing felt real yet. Everything had the quality of a dream and of a camping trip where I would soon be back to "normal." Normal as I now know it was years away.

I had made it to Uganda – in Fort Portal – but I did not really know what my next steps should be. My loneliness was a physical pain. I didn't realize that following my intuition would be such a lonely experience. I was frightened to shop in markets and did not know what shops had what in them. I felt shy to go into the shops. I spent many hours within the house trying to learn how to cook and do things without modern conveniences. A neighbor man used to come by, constantly begging. Neighbor kids banged on the door, demanding food and anything I would give. Clothes left on the line were stolen. I spent these weeks in prayer, searching for what God had in mind for me.

My first Easter, I woke up with a migraine headache and did not go to church. Rev. Sam drove to the Cathedral by himself but made it clear that he expected a good dinner for the holiday. He sulked when I didn't comply. Instead, I walked in the hills, and there I met Rev. Charles. He invited me to his parents' home on Easter Monday. I accepted with gratitude. Rev. Sam became furious and refused to come. He ordered me not to go. I ignored him and had a great day with wonderful, friendly people. They lived about 20 miles out of Fort Portal on Kasese Road which runs along the base of the Rwenzori Mountains. They were partly up in the mountains. We traveled through lush shades of green, past flowers, small waterfalls and so many colorful birds. The monkeys set up a huge noise in groups in trees. Charles filled me in on stories of his childhood. In rainy weather, he and neighbor kids would slide down steep banks on banana leaves in the mud and then jump into a nearby stream to clean some of the mud off before heading home. Kids anywhere in the world can have fun. I feel kids here seem happier than so many kids in the developed world who have so much.

Rev. Sam traveled several times to Kampala working on the NGO papers while I stayed in Fort Portal, writing letters on an old, borrowed typewriter. A few times I went with him. Once he convinced me to go by myself with some of these papers because he thought a *mzungu* might have a better chance getting them accepted. Back then the road was almost a dirt path in places, and the trip took close to nine hours. During the rainy season, the matatu drivers sometimes ask all passengers to get out on a bigger hill and the men help push it while ladies and kids walked. For toilet breaks, they stop by open fields, and ladies just squat in the grass. Men have it so much easier.

Traveling by *matatu* and finding my way around Kampala was a huge learning experience. The first months were so scary and lonely that I would travel out to the Besiniya school in Mukono, an hour outside of Kampala, to use Simeon's email. I desperately needed to connect with friends from outside.

Sam Mutabazi, who lived in Kampala, and I became friends. He regularly had an assortment of kids and relatives in and out but always made room for me in his small apartment. He lived in an area I then thought was a slum. Later, having seen real slums, I realized that it just was a rough neighborhood. No other *mzungu* was ever seen in that area, but people all treated me well. I confided in him over my growing concerns about working with Rev. Sam. Sam was supportive. I would be welcomed in his village in the South if things didn't work out. I felt, however, that Fort Portal was where I belonged.

Things continued up and down when I became sick with high fevers. I was chilled and sweating at the same time. Nausea hit in waves followed by abdominal pains and diarrhea. Rev. Sam decided to take that time and travel to Kampala. I was so sick that I didn't get out of bed for food or anything. A wonderful neighbor found me so delirious I didn't know where I was. She got me to a doctor.

Feeling lost and scared, I thank God for sending some friendly people. Ivan and Grace Byaruhanga and their children lived nearby. They stepped up to help. Ivan taught school while Grace ran one of the many small shops, maybe 8' by 10', selling of a bit of everything. They were low key, never begging me for money or help with the kids. Once I improved, they had me over a few times for what they called "evening tea" which was more like a meal in sort of a British way. The tea is mixed with sugar and milk, and they add *japaties* – a flat bread type food--along with some hard-boiled eggs, pieces of liver, roasted peanuts called "gnuts" and bananas and fruits. There is no way to walk away from local "tea" hungry. They were caring and friendly, along with some other neighbors. When I started my NGO, Ivan joined as a board member. He, Grace, and I are still friends.

This was my first of many bouts with malaria. Malaria is borne by mosquitos – impossible to avoid! I had attack after attack until finally my body seemed to adjust. Now I get a mild case a few times a year, and I will forever live with hearing loss. In the early years, quinine was the only medicine available for malaria. I would be given large amounts with an IV drip because I was so ill. Quinine is known to cause deafness, and now there are better medicines available.

That first time, however, was debilitating. I couldn't eat, dress, even get to the bathroom, more a latrine outside. In Uganda, if you need to use a bathroom you ask for a toilet or latrine. Otherwise, you are led to an area made with a reed wall and flat rocks on the ground where the host brings you a basin with water to bathe. I learned this this the hard way. When I was finally up and around, I received a fax from Sam Mutabazi who heard I was left alone and sick. He invited me to his village, asking that I allow his wife to care for me while I got stronger. We had no phones in those days except for the post office where faxes came in. I replied I would enjoy that. We arranged a time to meet in the town of Mbarara, about five hours south of Fort Portal. Then we headed together with his older daughter to his town of Kanungu, about another four hours southwest. A more direct route would take us across the foothills of the mountains and through the Kigezi Game Reserve. Much as I would have liked to see gorillas, this was not the time.

Rev. Sam was not at all happy with that decision.

When Sam and I connected, we drove another five hours to his village. The area was in the high hills. As dusk arrived, we were driving on a road cut into a cliff. Suddenly, a man with a gun jumped into the road pointing it at us. Sam screamed for his daughter and me to duck down and at the driver to step on the gas. The armed man was so startled that he never got off a shot but dove for the edge of the road as the driver tried to run him over. The funny part of this story is that the others in the car were unphased by the incident, talking and laughing after the incident as if it never happened.

In another 20 minutes we drove into Sam's home where his wife had prepared a lovely room for me with a vase of new flowers beside the bed and dinner waiting. I was hungry and enjoyed a great meal, then slept for the next 15 hours. I spent eight days sleeping and resting and praying and thinking. I decided to leave Rev. Sam and find a place of my own. I resented how he expected me to care for him, plus I could no longer live with his temper and moods. Time for another change. Sometimes you just need a little time and space, which illness will force you to take, to reset and refocus yourself. Sam and his wife and family were lovely and supportive and continued to make it clear that if I wished I could come there to work with them.

The priest who owned the house I was living in at the time with Rev. Sam decided he wanted to make good money from the *mzungu*. He demanded six months' rent in advance. I did not have it. I had been sending out letters to US friends looking for sponsors for students who Rev. Sam suggested we help. The only telephone available for individual calls was at the post office. We didn't have email, but the post office had a fax machine. I was sending out faxes trying to get more of my money wired to Uganda, but that also was a huge problem. When the priest demanded the advance, I faxed home again in a panic as I did not even have enough for much food.

When I returned from Sam Mutabazi's village recovered from malaria, I told Rev. Sam that I needed to find a less expensive place to live – without him. That did NOT go over well, but I was becoming stronger and more self-confident. I started asking around, trying to find out where I might move. Within that same time frame, I met the bishop of the Rwenzori Diocese Church of Uganda, located in Fort Portal on a campus often referred to as Kabarole Hill, for the land it occupies. The man who sent out the faxes must have told him a *mzungu* in town was having a difficult time financially.

Bishop Eustace Kamanyire came to the house with his wife. They were friendly, and I served them tea. The bishop asked if I had seen any of the tourist areas and invited me to come to Queen Elizabeth Park the next day along with Rev. Sam.

Queen Elizabeth Park is a fantastic place to bring guests. On game drives, I have seen lions, water buffalo, Uganda kobs, and many wilder beasts. You can take the Kazingo Channel boat ride. The channel joins Lake George with Lake Edward. From the boat, one sees hippos, crocodiles and elephants along with more bird species than anyone can imagine. The park is like what most people envision Africa with dry and hot savannas. It is only about 3 hours from my house. The drive there is also spectacular as we drive along the base of the Rwenzori Mountain chain before descending to the rift valley. If the weather is clear, we can see the glacier and snow on top of the mountain called Margarita.

Most of our major roads are built by Chinese companies, and there are quite a few Chinese nationals living in Fort Portal. The roads can be a bit rough, but because it is a tourist destination, they are kept up a bit better. There is even a shop now that looks like they are trying to imitate Walmart but way smaller. There is no quality control in Uganda, so buyers need to be a bit careful.

I often take sponsors and visiting friends to the park. On one trip there, I opted out of the game drive to have some time to myself. While enjoying the beauty of the park, an elephant walked up into our campground. The Ugandan workers ran away and yelled to me to run inside the camp's hostel. Being the stubborn person I am, I stayed to watch, sitting on a low wall to see what this lone elephant was up to. After washing her face with some soapy water that a cleaning lady left behind, the elephant wandered over to me. She looked so lonely and sad. She reached her trunk to me which I rubbed as I talked with her.

"You poor dear...you look lonely, sweetie...where are your friends? Don't let us scare you...that's a good girl." I used the tone I'd used since childhood to talk with animals. I have always struggled to connect with humans but felt right at home with animals.

She let me rub her trunk for a bit then wandered off. My visitors returned, we packed and headed down the road to where the car was parked. I remembered that I left shampoo in the bathroom, so I headed back to the cabin. As I came out, my elephant came around the corner, and she followed me like a puppy to the car. As I was about to get in, she kissed my back with her muddied trunk, and I turned around and gave her a quick hug. Many people don't believe my elephant story, but I have pictures. Later, a game warden told me her name was Mary. She was orphaned and villagers helped feed her until she got older. That explained why she was sad and lonely but trusting with me.

On a separate trip to Queen Elizabeth Park, I met the bishop's driver Charles Agaba, a sweet and kind giant of a man and black as coal. During our first trip together, Charles answered my many questions about Queen Elizabeth Park and pointed out the sights. We stopped along the road for me to see a group of baboons. I left the door open while trying to get some pictures, and a clever baboon stole our lunch. Rev. Sam, who'd been sulking, was furious - as if I did it intentionally. As annoyed as I was with him, I had to laugh to myself about being robbed by a monkey!

The day was fantastic. I took several rolls of film of animals roaming freely among the savannah grasses and bush. I was getting on famously with Charles as he taught me how to spot a warthog in their camouflage coloring. The bishop was a lot of fun, but Rev. Sam behaved like a kid we should have left at home. My only disappointment as we left was that I hadn't seen a single elephant. I love elephants, and I really wanted to see some in the wild on this trip.

As we were headed out of the park, we spotted a huge bull elephant near the road. Charles grinned at me in the mirror and stopped as I rolled down the window for a photo. Just as I rolled the window and was aiming my camera, the elephant became quite upset and let out a trumpet, easily heard a mile away. He came charging straight toward the truck. The bishop was screaming, "*Genda! Genda!*" (Go!!! Go!!!) to Charles. Unfortunately, I froze instead of taking a picture as the trunk came right in the window close to my face. Charles started up the engine of the truck, wheels a spinning, which shot stones behind and momentarily stopped the elephant. He then started chasing us. He could run fast as the truck would go, and Charles changed from gear to gear as fast as possible, Meanwhile, if a black man could turn white, Rev. Sam surely would have. He was crumpled in the corner of the seat, shaking all over with fear. The bishop was scolding Charles harshly, telling him he should have known better. I looked at Charles in the rear-view mirror, and we were trying hard not to laugh which made Rev. Sam even more angry. At least I saw my first wild elephant. I later learned that he was an outcast from his heard and grumpy. He seldom was seen near roadways, but local people were aware of him and careful.

When we reached Fort Portal, the rains were pouring

down. Both the road to where I lived and the road to the bishop's house were undrivable. We stayed in a junky hotel. The only food left was some old rice. I had just filled my mouth when Charles smirked and said quietly, "want to see an elephant?" I choked and blew half-chewed rice all over as Charles and I fell apart in laughter. Years later, I shared that story with my sister. She made a necklace for me and a keychain for Charles from two small elephant decorations. Charles and I always had them to remember the day we met. Unique individuals can make true and lasting friends.

That was the start of a fast and dear friendship. I try to remember Charles as he was then. He died of AIDS in 2010. Our program built him and his family including a wife, two sons, and daughter, Sarah a new house. It was a local style wattle home with an iron roof. Many homes have thatching for roofs. However, thatching smells, lets rodents and bugs get in, and never lasts long. Anyone who can possibly manage puts a metal roof on a house, even if they must skip many a meal to do so. The strong house we built had cement plastered mud walls and three bedrooms with a kitchen and latrine outside. Sarah was admitted to our Manna Rescue Home a few years later and has now been adopted by a family in the US. Charles' oldest son, James is finishing university with the help of Sarah's adoptive family. As we were finishing the house, Charles was admitted to the hospital as a living skeleton. Watching someone die of AIDS is horrible as they almost disintegrate while alive. Relegated to a communal room, people were coming into the room to stare at him because he looked so incredibly ghastly. He begged me with tears in his eyes to take him home to die. My efforts to meet his request became a battle. The hospital accused me of killing him. They relented when I asked if he would live if he stayed. Finally, I carried him like a baby to the car as he weighed almost nothing. He rallied once at home, and lived three more months, with dignity.

Months later, the bishop offered me an apartment attached to the old, formerly British house on Kabarole Hill where the Cathedral was located. The run-down house had electricity, which was a blessing, but it had no running water. The neighbors were all friendly, and better yet, spoke English. The reverend and his family living in the main part of the house were friendly and welcomed me. Behind the house, an elderly and some-what crazy lady lived in an old hut. My area consisted of a large sitting (living) room and a nice bedroom. I had a bathroom, with no running water, and a kitchen the size of a large closet. I did not have a refrigerator and only a few shelves. I cooked on a small paraffin stove. The little kitchen sink drained out to the side of the house. I purchased some local furniture and bought a nice bed from some *bzungu* who were leaving it behind.

I was finally living on my own and getting more comfortable with the local people who were so very welcoming to me. I tried hard to follow the Ugandan culture of serving tea when guests dropped in and shar-ing food if they dropped in while I happened to be eat-ing. This happened so frequently, I found myself eating quickly or in my bedroom so as not to be seen.

High Hope, the NGO I built with Rev. Sam, slowly gained momentum. We provided tuition for students and care for orphans. I organized the student lists and kept the accounts.

I was making some decisions on my own for students who needed help in the program and spending a lot of time writing potential donors. I had a small office outside of the main house which originally was a storeroom. I met many shady characters there as well as wonderful people.

Including my second son.

Chapter 12

Just Love,
No Matter What

This precious life began in a thunderstorm. Someone running across a washed-out road found him as a newborn. The Samaritan rushed him to a hospital where a lady who had a stillbirth took him in. Pulled from the water, they named him Moses.

I was brand new in Fort Portal when Moses Magezi came to me with an older lady asking for help with secondary school fees. He so desired schooling that he commuted from 20 kilometers away. One of my early decisions, taking on Moses angered Rev. Sam who thought only he should make decisions.

One night I was out on the lawn barefoot, admiring the stars and listening to the wonderful African night sounds, rustling breeze, settling birds, frogs, insects. From one instant to the next, a burning sensation stinged up my legs. Hundreds of army ants ran up my calves, eating me all along on the way. I screamed and ran, slapping my legs. In the dark as there was no power that night, I raced for the bathroom. My legs dripped with blood from the ant bites. I jumped into the tub only to feel a squishing sensation. The tub began filling with the same ants coming up through the drain. I really started screaming then. Moses understood what was happening and brought in handfuls of burned charcoal dust from where we cooked. I had ripped off my skirt and was frantically trying to pull ants off without much success when Moses started rubbing the charcoal on me. The ants fell off immediately.

Moses kept rubbing in charcoal dust until all the ants were gone. By then I was shaking and bleeding and quite worked up. I had thrown my skirt into the tub of ants, so I went and grabbed another. The kettle had been boiling on the stove, so we poured boiling water in the tub, ridding it of ants, and then we plugged the opening. I learned later that the ants can kill a cow and often will kill a chicken if it unable to escape. Amazing and scary.

Fighting off ants wasn't my only excitement. One day, I visited a village called Karambi, about 15 kilometers outside of Fort Portal along what was then a dirt road. I went to pick up videos of local instruments and singing I hoped to present during my first fundraising trip and spent more time at the church than I planned. I returned home in near dark with a thunderstorm fast approaching. The wind whipped clouds of dust, and the sky filled with impressive, forked lightning. I was worried because I did not like traveling after dark. A half kilometer down the road, the rain came down in torrents. Just then, a very pregnant lady rushed to the side of the road frantically waving me down. I stopped, and she climbed in.

"Irraro, irraro," she said, pointing to her stomach.

"Virika?" I asked, understanding *irrarro* to mean hospital and Virika being the nearest.

She nodded then screamed as she had a contraction.

By then it was completely dark, the storm raged, and the road was slippery. I drove as quickly and carefully as I could.

Suddenly, a man appeared, rushing on a bicycle. The woman conveyed he was her husband. I stopped, and when he saw his wife in the car, he threw his bike in the back of my truck and climbed inside despite the storm.

We were nearing the hospital when the woman again screamed, and her body went straight. I realized that the baby must be coming. I pulled over, ran around the truck, and opened the door just in time to catch the baby. The only light came from the lightning. The baby let out a squeal but was still attached by the umbilical cord. I took off my coat and wrapped the baby, placing the baby in the woman's arms. The husband, who was drunk, pulled out a dirty knife to cut the cord. I refused to let him use it to cut the cord and had to roughly order him into the back of the truck, and then drove the rest of the way to the hospital.

When we arrived, everything was dark – no electricity tonight. After about 10 minutes, which seemed like forever, staff came to cut the cord and took the mom and baby inside. The nurse translated that the father asked me to drive him back into town to get needed supplies. Unhappy with the idea of going all the way back with a drunk man who could not even talk with me, I agreed. The storm had slowed to a drizzle, but the road was slippery. In Karambi, the man got out and disappeared. I looked for a place to turn around and almost slid off the road doing it. I then waited another 20 minutes before the man came back with a bundle for his wife.

You may wonder why I'd risk returning in the rain to the town of Karambi. When I arrived in Uganda, and to some extent still today, patients had to bring their own mattress and bedding to the hospital. Families are responsible for bringing linens, plastic basins, and anything else their loved ones might need during a hospital stay.

Once I was with two *bzungu*, one who had visited before and adopted a child from my program, and the other on her first visit. We were shopping in the market for trinkets for them to take home to relatives when I took a terrible fall and badly cracked my head on the pavement. I hit so hard that one of my hearing aids flew out plus my bag went flying. Immediately a crowd swarmed all over with advice and help from different people. In Kampala, people would likely steal my things, but in Fort Portal the rather noisy crowd all seemed to know and want to help me. When I came to, I asked two *bzungu* who were visiting to phone my physician, Dr. Henry, and another friend who could drive us to the hospital.

At the hospital, I was taken to a partially open area with rooms on the perimeters. Each room had one light bulb hanging on a wire while the open area had no lights. The dull grey interior had only cement floors splattered with bird droppings, broken brick walls, and open beams. Birds were flying to nest here and there as night approached. Clothes lines crossed in haphazard fashion with old bed sheets, towels, and a variety of garments dripping onto the dirty floor. Patient rooms were decrepit and dirty. You could smell disinfectant, body odor, food waste, and an old overflowing toilet. I was placed on an examination table in a treatment room along the perimeter. The corner of the room held old plastic bottles, old papers, and a haphazard bunch of boxes with different equipment. Dr. Henry opened sterile water and needles to sew me up. My head was spinning, and I felt cold water running down my neck. There was no medicine available for pain, but the area being stitched was numbed. All of it seemed quite normal until I realized that one of my visitors was freaking out, saying she had to go home – to the US, NOT my house. My visitor was so, so shocked with what I now consider normal hospital conditions.

These were the kinds of conditions existing for the expectant mother on that fateful night. On returning to the hospital, we found her with the baby sleeping in a small box beside the bed. I peeked to catch a glimpse of the baby girl. Heading back to the house, I was exhausted but happy to know all was well with the mother and daughter. The mother did not know who I was, but she named her baby Carol. Seventeen years later, my namesake appeared at my office. She had asked many people about the lady who helped deliver her. Carol is now in first year of university.

By comparison, birthing an NGO was more harrowing.

Bishop Kamanyire decided he should join me on my fundraising trip. I was so lonely and homesick, it hit like a physical pain at times. With the program already started and myself in a more stable living situation, I decided to travel and raise more funds. I sent out many letters and was invited to speak in both England and the US. I was energized as I worked out a travel plan. I welcomed the credibility the bishop's presence would give to my work.

I was at the diocesan offices, finalizing some paper-work late in the evening before leaving the following day for the UK when Rev. Sam came into the office.

"Who do you think you are?" he yelled. "I brought you here. You do what I say!"

"I'm doing this for the program," I tried to interject.

"You think you can steal the bishop, poison people against me?" he yelled getting even louder, flailing his arms, filling the tiny space.

His horrible rage scared me.

"What's going on?" Charles stepped in. "Are you

OK, *Adyeeri*?"

"No, no I'm not." I said.

"She's fine. Get out," Rev. Sam ordered.

"Please, Charles, stay!"

"I'm not going anywhere, sir," Charles said as he planted his huge frame inside the door.

"I'm not finished with you," said Rev. Sam leaving in a fury.

Charles walked me home, and I locked my door securely for the night. That's the final straw, I thought to myself.

On the way to the city, I penned a letter saying I would no longer work for High Hope. My upcoming fundraising trip would be for my own program. Once again, I must go it alone.

Despite armies of ants and my battle with Rev. Sam, my work brought me great joy. I had the chance to teach American baseball to the girls from the female secondary (high school) boarding school. One Sunday after church service, a shy teenage girl, Rose Katwesige, who'd seen me playing baseball with other girls, asked to talk to me about problems she was having trying to go to school. She was so polite and a bit scared. I invited her home to have some tea and talk. She explained that she was in Senior One in a girl's school but could not raise enough money to continue. She said that she really wanted an education. I promised to go to her school on the following Monday to talk with her teachers. If they said she was a serious student, I agreed that I would help her.

Rose was the 13th and last child in her family. By the time she was born, her mother was tired. She was raised by her sister who wanted a baby but could not get pregnant. When Rose was 12, her sister died from cancer, and her sister's husband had already died of AIDS. That's when she learned that the old couple she had always believed to be her grandparents were actually her parents. She moved in with all the kids and some other orphans living in a small mud shack with little food or care, sleeping on the dirt floor with around twenty children piled up. The kids would go to the garbage pit for meals, chasing away rats from any pieces they could find. The new life was a shock.

Rose's sister had inspired her to get an education. She was already in her last year of primary school. She managed to work for neighbors for a little money for school fees and basic needs. When she finished Primary 7, she got hired as a house girl by a wealthy, Indian family in Kampala. There she worked for a year to earn money for secondary. She knew she couldn't make it while living at home, so she entered a girls' boarding school after one year in Kampala. The full year's wages got used up with first term—3 terms in a year. That is when she came to talk with me.

I went to her school the next day and the sisters—a Catholic school – said Rose was a remarkable girl who should be helped. I started paying her school fees, and she continued working for the sisters on weekends and evenings for other income. After Senior 4, she attended a business school for secretarial training. She finished in two years but found it hard to get a job. I was working without any staff, so I hired her. We had some great times and laughs. She got my sarcastic ways and got pretty good at sarcasm herself. She is now married to a British man and has two lovely girls. They come back to visit, and she is still the sweet girl who became like my daughter.

Rose is one of many great girls who came through my program and warmed my heart.

And then there was Christine.

Chapter 13

A Rant, A Threat and A Poisoning?

The trip with Bishop Eustace took us to England, Washington DC, New York, North Carolina, Florida, Colorado, California and finally home to Maui. I arrived home exhausted, but the trip was successful. I stayed longer in Maui for some minor surgery on my face. The metals in my cheeks were causing pain and problems.

We had left in November, and I flew back to Uganda in February.

"I am back in Uganda where I feel I belong. Many things are coming up at once. Bishop Eustace wants to have an NGO instead of working through the diocese. I agree but already have some worries about the advisability of that.

He also has thoughts of fixing up some old build-ings in a nearby village and fixing an older mud house for me to live in." *Journal entry, February 1997*

With some reluctance, I went along with the bishop's plan. I was now running my program alone. Rev. Sam took the small pick-up I had purchased. I had put it in the NGO's name so I couldn't argue. I was on foot or a *boda* taxi, working on building up a childcare program. Under the Anglican Church of Uganda, I developed Child Care Outreach. I converted a small room where I was living into an office. I already had several kids who I had started with school fees and took on several more.

I didn't have a lot of money for myself as I refused to take any sponsorship money to live on, so I was struggling to get enough food. On thinking back, I feel this was a good time for my health. I arrived in Uganda suffering frequent, severe migraines. Having so little money, I was living on vegetables. I think the diet, heavy on fresh foods and free of the processing and artificial preservatives of Western food (not to mention my addiction to fast food), helped clear my body. I have since been migraine free.

I had not been living long in Fort Portal before I invited a young woman to stay with me in my new home. Christine was an orphan introduced to me by Rev. Sam and, she was a student in a boarding school some distance from Fort Portal. I paid for her school fees, fed and clothed her. I set a curtain at the end of the sitting room with a bed behind it for her room.

Even as I cared for one of his wards, Rev. Sam's and my work were disentangling, and the community knew it.

"Be careful," Patrick Isingoma, one of the bishop's drivers, warned me one day. "Christine's seeing a lot of Rev. Sam."

"She's working for him," I said.

"Maybe," he said cautiously. "Rev. Sam's still terribly angry with you."

"He'll get over it," I tried to believe.

"You're not safe," Patrick said, leaving me to worry.

On a Saturday morning, Rev. Sam came to the house.

"We have to talk," he said.

"We can talk in the office on Monday."

"It's urgent. We need to talk now," he demanded.

I let him in. Immediately, he started raging.

"Uganda and Fort Portal are mine," he yelled. "We can't both live here."

"I have every right to live wherever I want," I said stubbornly.

"I won't stand for it," he shouted.

"Leave," I said, as calmly as I could.

"No woman is going to tell me what to do."

"This woman is," I said, and shoved him out. I pulled the door shut and locked it.

He stomped back up the road. "I'm going to finish her," he told all the diocesan staff he passed. Women here are considered inferior and must fight for land ownership and many other things. I am working hard with my girls in the program now to let them know they deserve the same rights as men and do not need to be subservient. I have seen huge progress in my 20 plus years.

That same week, I went into Kampala to do some work and get some money from the bank to buy a small car. Bishop Eustace was helping me with the transfer of ownership, and he received a message from John Katuramu that Katuramu needed to see me. I had repaid the loan on the truck, so I did not know what he wanted. Katuramu owned a huge business and fancy apartment on the third story. I walked up the stairs, noticing the security cameras watching me. An armed guard let me into a luxurious room where Katuramu waited, then stayed standing in the doorway.

"Have a seat," said Katuramu, more of an order than a request.

"Thank you," I said, sitting on the edge of a couch.

"Why did you leave Sam and High Hope?" he demanded, referring to the Rev. Sam.

"Sam knows why I left. He knows exactly why I left. I'd rather keep it between us," I answered.

"I disagree. I take a particular interest in my friends," he said.

"I have no concern with you or your friends," I said politely.

"I order you to go back," he said. "I expect you to stand by the arrangement made when I loaned you the money for the truck."

"I appreciate your assistance, Mr. Katuramu. That's why I paid you back fully in less than a month."

Katuramu was breathing hard and sweating, still I persisted.

"The truck remains with High Hope. And my business with Sam and High Hope is my business."

"You are playing a dangerous game with your life," he said in a terribly cold and controlled voice.

"I see no reason to stay and listen to this," I replied and stood up.

"SIT DOWN," he bellowed. "No one walks out on me."

"It looks like I'll be the first," I said and turned to walk out.

The guard with the MK 47 looked at him and then me. I walked past him and down the steps. When I reached the sidewalk, I was shaking so badly I could hardly stand up.

I headed back to Fort Portal and chose not to worry, much. Bishop Kamanyire was horrified when he heard that I had defied Katuramu. "You were very, very foolish," he said. "You could have been shot then and there."

The following Sunday when I returned from church, I found my apartment trashed. The culprits stole almost everything I owned, including mattresses, bedding, pots and pans, radio, clothes, my papers, even the electric bills. Though in a terrible shock, I was overwhelmed with the loving and caring response of everyone in the diocese. They came around and prayed with me and comforted me.

Most notable, nothing belonging to Christine was stolen, and she had gone to be with some friends right after church instead of coming back with me.

The break-in was a terrible shock. Christine became unfriendly, casting disheartening doubt on her possible involvement. And this was my first experience with the police in Uganda, and I soon learned they would offer little help.

Often criminals make it neither to jail nor a judge. When I worked in the church office on Kabarole Hill, a thief broke in and took a computer, camera and some money. A couple of days later, I heard a lot of yelling. A large group held a man who lived nearby in a shack. The stupid man was trying to steal a generator. When he was caught, they found my camera and other things in his possession. After I identified my things, the group started kicking and beating the man. I jumped into the fray and demanded they stop. At first, they refused. I continued yelling, and they backed off. The police finally arrived, and one cop picked up a chain from the ground and swung it at the man. The thief started bleeding on the cop who only got angrier. I ordered him to stop as he moved to beat the man. The cop complained about blood stains, so I told him how to wash them out. He then claimed that his work made him "thirsty." I pulled out some money and asked Rose to run to the kiosk for a soda. "But, Ms. Carol," she started to say, "that's not what…" I gave her a look, and she ran for the soda. Cop and thief left, neither too happy, and I don't know the outcome.

If a policeman or anyone in service says that they would like some tea, they are asking for money or a bribe. I learned this saying in my first year. I parked my car at a girl's boarding school behind locked gates. I lived just down the road from the school. I arrived home one evening just at dark on a windy, rainy and chilly night. I parked, and as I hurried out the gates someone called to me.

"Madam," the gate man stopped me, "every night your motor car sleeps here safely. Some tea would be good.»

"Yes, it does, and I'm grateful to you for watching it."

I walked home, feeling the chill. I decided to fix us some tea with much sugar and milk as they like it here. I also wrapped up some cake. I hurried back with the thermos.

"Here," I said, handing him the treats. "It must be a cold job as watchman all night."

I knew the long watch was lonely and sometimes scary from the time I'd spent as a night guard myself in Hawaii.

"Um, uh, thank you," he said slowly, taking the items.

The next day I told a teacher friend at the school that they really should have some place the poor man could get tea on cold nights, relating my encounter with the guard. My friend laughed and laughed. It's still a joke to this day.

I did learn quite a bit more about how things

worked. When a stone from a large lorry smashed my windscreen (truck and windshield in British English), it shattered into hundreds of tiny pieces. No missing windscreen was going to stop me. I had to get to a container of relief supplies in urgent need at a displacement camp. As I turned off the main road, a fat, gap-toothed cop flagged me to stop. She sashayed over to my car.

"Madam, you do not have a windscreen," she said. I had to bite my tongue to not respond equally sarcastic.

"I have a new one on order from Kampala. Mine shattered this morning."

"I do not see your insurance sticker," she said.

I opened the glove box and pulled out a plastic bag filled with tiny pieces of glass that had the green sticker on it.

"I'm going to the insurance office and get a new one once I get a new windscreen," I explained.

She looked at me and said, "I'm getting frustrated," while rubbing her thumb and forefinger together.

"This situation has me frustrated, as well," I said, pretending I didn't have a clue what she wanted.

"Madam, I'm hungry," she said.

I looked at my watch and said," lunchtime, I know. I'm hungry too."

By then she was steaming. "If I stay hungry, we might just go to the police station together."

"We go," I said and pushed open the passenger door.

She glared at me and said, "Get out of here and don't let me see you again!"

I had to work hard to not laugh until I got out of

sight, but I avoided her from then on.

Bribery is common for big and little things. I try hard to never pay a bribe, but there have been a couple of situations that I felt cornered and couldn't bluff my way out. In Kampala, my then field officer David Tumwiine was driving when two cops jumped into the car as we turned out of a shopping mall. They said he was driving badly which was crazy as the whole city seems to drive badly. David explained I was headed to an appointment for an MRI. The police told him to drive to the police station, that my appointment was not their concern. I pulled out two 10,000 USh---about $3---- and asked if they might just go get a cup of tea instead. They agreed, and we drove away. If I had not, we would have wasted a lot of time and likely been hit with a much bigger fine than the smaller tea.

Each situation needs to be considered. If I had given in to the female cop in my home region, the word would spread that I was good for some tea. Police are critically underpaid. If a police person is helpful to me, I will give a thank you payment. The minute they ask, I get stubborn. Life here can be funny. When I get together with other *bzungu,* we have a great time exchanging stories. Some *bzungu* get angry and that anger sends them on a plane headed home. I think a sense of humor is really needed to continue with the work we do here.

Perhaps it took me a while to get the gist of the bribery lingo because everyone here is simultaneously polite and direct. I was giving a presentation in a fundraiser in Ireland when at the end a man came to me and said,

"I love your talks as you are so innocently, politically incorrect." He didn't explain in what ways I was not correct. Living in Uganda makes a person forget how touchy people are about words in developed countries. Here they often say it as they see it. For instance, "Madam, you are getting quite fat." Often descriptions are direct such as "the crippled boy," "the lady with the sagging face," "the deaf or blind person," no put down or insult intended. A retarded girl at the orphanage I run is called "retarded" here. That is a fact and not an insult as saying that she is a "retard" in an ugly way would be. In fact, she gets more hugs than others as she is very loving. Ugandans also use skin variations such as "the black one," "the tan one" or even "the half cast," all descriptions are accepted here without problems. I have an obese friend who came to me in tears because someone said how fat she was. A Ugandan friend standing nearby asked her why she was upset. "Fat is good. You will live longer if food gets gone," she said. Age is also highly respected. I am called a *mukaikuru* which means old lady, and often people call me "mama."

About two weeks after the theft at my home, one of the bishop's drivers, Patrick Isingoma, told me he saw Christine go to Rev. Sam's house sometimes after I was in bed, and Rev. Sam even came back with her a couple of times.

"Christine, what's going on with you and Rev. Sam?" I confronted her.

"You're not my mother," she said. "You can't tell me what to do,"

"As long as you live with me, you need to follow my rules." I said.

"I'm free to do as I wish," she said.

"You're free to do what you want as soon as you decide to leave," I replied.

Christine sulked and refused to speak to me. About five days later, she came to my office and asked if she could talk.

"I'm so sorry, Mama Carol, for acting like a child."

"Oh, Christine," I said, wanting to return to our camaraderie.

"Please forgive me," she said.

"I certainly do," I said. She gave me a hug.

"I want to cook you something special," she smiled, leaving for the apartment.

When I walked in, she presented a fried chicken dinner with fresh veggies and gravy with mashed potatoes. Everything was delicious, and I enjoyed the large, home-cooked meal.

That night I started throwing up badly. The next morning, I had someone take me to Virika, the Catholic hospital. They diagnosed a bad stomach flu and gave me several medicines.

When I returned, Christine was absent. I was sort of glad to be rid of her while I was so sick.

That night, my face swelled like a rancid melon about to burst. I went back to Virika. They suggested I go to Kampala for more tests. Lindsey, a visitor from Hawaii, went with me. One doctor said it appeared that I had ingested some sort of poison, but I said that could not be. They ran several inconclusive tests and sent me home with more medicines. Within days, I was suffering badly from diarrhea. Bishop Eustace recommended I fly to Nairobi. I was so weak I agreed.

Concerned with how I looked, Patrick drove me and Lindsey to Kampala that same day. The doctor in Kampala agreed that I should fly to Nairobi. Patrick sat by my bed all night. By morning, I could no longer walk. Patrick got me to the airport, and an airport ambulance shuttled me to the plane. The airline refused to take me without a nurse. Lindsey claimed to be a nurse, so they allowed me on. In Nairobi, the pilot phoned ahead. The attendants quickly took me through customs and ushered me to the waiting taxi. On the way to the hospital, a police officer stopped the taxi over some vehicle problem. I waited miserably while the driver and police argued. When I finally reached the hospital, I was admitted to the casualty department where they immediately started a drip. My organs were shutting down.

In the casualty, I met a lady, Carmen, whose husband was admitted for the flu. Lindsey left, unhappy with being "stuck" in a Nairobi Hospital. Carmen befriended me and visited often, even after her husband was discharged. At her home, she had internet, highly uncommon. She emailed my brother Henry.

The Nairobi staff couldn't diagnose my problem. After ten days and many tests, they suggested a colostomy, believing my lower intestine badly damaged. Henry offered to have me come back to the US to stay with him and decide from there. Bishop Eustace flew over from Uganda. Between him and Carmen, they helped me get my tickets and get to the airport.

The trip was a nightmare. I staggered through airports and flights in a fog. In a British airport, I almost got arrested when I asked a nice-looking older couple to please watch my luggage while I used the restroom. They loudly refused. I staggered in with my suitcases. When I came out, airport security waited for me. I showed them that I had not left my suitcases, and after a lecture they left me alone.

I finally reached Rochester, NY. I had to wait for Henry, and I collapsed on some chairs in the lobby. When he finally arrived, he took me directly to a doctor who offered only minimal assistance because I lacked insurance. Henry took me to his home and set me up on a sofa bed in his office. I remember some inconclusive visits where the doctors suspected that I had Crohn's disease. At least I was no longer dangerously sick.

A friend in California believed I could access insurance there, so I finally flew out to stay with her. No luck – I didn't even see a doctor. Friends from Maui said they could get me covered with Kaiser Insurance from their policy, so a week after arriving in California, I was again on a plane.

The good news – the doctors in Maui were able to help. The bad news - I moved from one place to another with different people taking me in. Everyone has their own life and their own problems. No one plans for a long visit from a sick friend. Thankfully, I had many good friends. I ended up staying in Maui for 6 months. While there, I contacted the Episcopal Relief Services who organized a 60-foot container for me to bring back to Uganda. I had continued following situations with the ADF war, and things were horrific. I used my down time sorting and packing the container with a lot of donated items from Maui well-wishers. The container was then shipped to Oakland, California, where I spent another two weeks to finish filling the huge container. I headed back to Uganda on Thanksgiving Day.

When I returned to Fort Portal, Christine was gone. I had to work around Rev. Sam. He eventually moved to the US where he heads a parish. However, I recently had the pleasure of seeing him again. I was in church when the priest said to welcome from America the Rev. Sam. I felt a shock. I last saw him over 20 years ago. He visited Uganda a couple of times, but we both avoided each other. Most of the older priests know that things were bad between us. A few suspect my sickness was in connection with him. The service proceeded with the usual singing and readings before the sermon. The Reverend Ezra Musobozi and I are friends who go way back. I believe he has a good idea of what went on between Rev. Sam and me. His sermon went into some detail about forgiveness and letting go being a form of freedom and on and on. Directed to me? When church let out, Rev. Sam reached the doorway before me. When I came out, he tried to leave, but some people had stopped to talk with him. I headed right to him, stuck my hand out and said, "Hello Sam." He stared at my hand as if it were a snake. Hiding the pause with a forced smile, he had to shake my hand with knowing congregants watching. I asked about his mother and his family in the States, and he relaxed considerably. I left wishing him a good day and headed to my car. Abwooli Rwakalembe, a dear friend, stopped me.

"I saw you greeting your best friend," she said, laughing.

"I'm a bit surprised at myself," I said.

"I could not believe what I was seeing," said Abwooli.

«And what was that sermon about?" I joined her levity.

I am not sure complete forgiveness has happened, but somehow, I felt quite good about the morning.

Chapter 14

Finding My Way

While I recovered in Hawaii, rebels attacked in Bundibugyo, Uganda. A friend was killed, and Bishop Eustice went missing. He had been confirming children into the church on a trip I was supposed to join. What a wrenching feeling being on the other side of the world and getting these horrifying stories. By 1997, the Ugandan war with the ADF (the Allied Democratic Forces in Uganda and Congo) was full blown, lasting at full speed until 2003. From 2003 up through 2006, it was pretty quiet in the Kabarole district. As silly as this sounds, the war situation was scarier to me when I was in the US and getting my information from the internet than when I'd been in Uganda. The war started in earnest around the time I was in the States for treatment. I read about atrocities and had nightmares. I wanted to get back as soon as I could as I worried about Moses and my other kids.

The rebels were causing terrible bloodshed and havoc. I wanted badly to get back to the kids and people I loved. What a huge relief to learn the bishop and his driver were safe. They hid in the mountains dressed poorly so as not to be recognized. An army helicopter rescued them after about a week.

I also remember hearing Mother Teresa died in the same week as Princess Diana died in a car wreck. I was angry that Mother Teresa's death seemed to take much less news space.

I needed to do something. I phoned the Episcopal Relief Fund in NYC, explaining the dire need caused by the war. They offered to ship a container of relief goods to Uganda if I would fill it. After much correspondence and phone calls, I managed to get a 20-foot container placed in the parking lot of a feed store owned by a good friend. Boxes and donations started flowing in. Between visits to the hospital, even flying a couple of times to Oahu for more elaborate tests, I sorted out donated goods and packed the container.

By November, I decided to return to Uganda. The doctors had been unable to diagnose my illness. They concluded I had serious lower intestine damage of unknown causes. They suggested a careful diet and warned me not to go back to Uganda. I had diarrhea daily but had learned to live with it. Friends from St. John's Church in Oakland, California, invited me to stop over and arranged for a 40-foot container to transfer what had been donated so far. With many more phone calls and assistance from a wonderful man named Sam Sause, donations filled the container and plans were made to ship it.

On Thanksgiving Thursday 1997, I finally headed to Fort Portal, to my home.

Not long after returning home, I learned Moses was having a difficult time finding a place to live. With permission, I arranged for a room with another boy on the other side of the house where I lived. As his term exams approached, that situation became disruptive, so I allowed him to move into my place in Christine's former space. I had no intention of having orphans live with me, but Moses was so helpful and so completely different than Christine that I ended up having him stay with me throughout his secondary school years.

Moses was a gift from God. Right away, he saw how foolish and trusting I was. He became my teacher about Uganda and its people. He also came to accept Christ and Christianity as the true way. I never pushed him. He shyly asked questions and came to his own decision regarding his faith.

By April of 1998, I was slowly growing my Child Care Outreach program through the Anglican Church of Uganda in the Kabarole Diocese in Fort Portal. One early morning, a priest came by and calmly announced that Edwin Bajenja had been murdered. Edwin and his wife Ellen were two of my first true friends in Fort Portal. I was in shock.

"It's God's plan," the priest said.

"No, it was Satan," I said through my fury at my friend's death, to the priest. "God does not plan evil."

I had never yelled at a priest before.

I found Ellen's house full of mourners. Edwin's body lay in a coffin in the living room. Ellen was devastated. I could not think of anything to say but to hug her and cry with her. The next day, over a thousand people attended the long Ugandan funeral, listening to the many speeches.

Edwin had discovered deep corruption at the international conservation NGO where he worked. The culprits broke into his house and shot him point blank in front of Ellen and his two little girls, ages 2 and 4. They only stole his briefcase which held all the evidence. Edwin's father had copies of everything in the briefcase, leading to the killer's capture, though he still managed to escape prison. To this day, Ellen and her girls are close friends. The girls are now grown and attending universities.

I continued building Child Care Outreach. I now lived with Moses, slowly learning more and more about Uganda, the people, the customs, and the land. Back then I had no staff except for some help from Moses who lived with me. Until listening to my cassettes, I'd forgotten that I did a lot of running around buying seeds and supplies for families to be able to plant more food. I had a lot of individual work with kids when I visited schools to see where they had problems plus paid school fees myself. I had a non-stop flow of people dropping in to visit. I was a novelty as about the only *mzungu* in the area.

Back then, I worried that I needed to be culturally

appropriate and serve tea and be nice to everyone. I was naive and made poor decisions.

One man convinced me he was helping a family in hiding from a rebel attack. He told me that the kids hid in the bush while their parents were killed by rebels. These things were happening, and I believed him. Moses became suspicious of all the "orphans" that this good Samaritan brought in. The stories were lies. The man told me that he and his wife were helping orphans in a small, thatched house he showed me a photo of. Even as gullible as I was, I questioned the lack of beds and clothes and other signs of daily life. He had trained the village kids to run to him whenever he came back with a *mzungu*. He would then claim that they were the orphans he assisted. I felt terrible because I had sent out a newsletter relating his false story. The saddest part of this deception, he was always praying and praising God. I often wonder how I would have made it without Moses' wisdom and help. Sadly, the fake Samaritan behavior continues to get visitors involved, even when there is real need.

Moses helped me see through the lies and deceptions employed when people think they can get some help. He also helped me let go of anger concerning such behavior. He made me realize that desperate people will try anything. People see *bzungu* as having unending money even when we don't. They know that we do not go to bed hungry after a day without food and that we have blankets and beds to sleep in and warm clothes to wear. That alone makes us rich.

One day, several months after Moses moved in with me, he came home carrying a small half-starved puppy.

"Can I keep him?" he asked.

"Moses, you're in school so much, I'll end up caring for it."

"Please, Gran," he said, with puppy eyes of his own.

"Ok, but you have to care for him, and keep up your studies."

"Yes, yes, of course," Moses said, delighted. "I'm calling him Rover because I read that is a dog's name."

I didn't argue. I really enjoyed having a pet again even though finding food for him daily was hard. There was no such thing as dog or cat food. People didn't believe me when I told them that in the US stores sold special food for pets. I found a local restaurant that allowed me to pick thrown away food daily if I left a bucket for them. That left me certain holidays when they were closed or slow days when I needed to find food for him. I found a butcher who would sell me meat scraps from the floor and sometimes a goat head to cook.

One day my regular butcher was not there. The man watching the shop didn't speak English.

"Embwa", I said – dog. Pointing to the case, I said "Enyama," – meat.

The man frowned and motioned me to wait. He went off and came back with another man.

"Madam, in Uganda, we do NOT eat dogs."

"What?! No, no, I want meat for my dog." I motioned taking meat and bending down to give it to an imaginary dog.

The men looked at my pantomime, at each other, at me then broke out laughing.

From then on, when I walked past that butcher he would call out, "Madam, do you want to eat dogs today?"

With Child Care Outreach in motion, I soon started searching for a place of my own to buy. In a village called Kasusu/Nsooro about 5 kilometers out of town, I found a half-acre of land with a dilapidated house left partially unbuilt at a fair price. A good friend and reverend at the church warned the village was not at all safe. I appreciated his concern. The bishop was also concerned, insulted that I rejected a house he had planned for me.

I have found that God always gives me a feeling of peace when I make a big decision. Without that peace, I do not go forward. I felt confident. I felt at peace with my decision.

I met an Irish missionary family, Norman and Isobel Jackson, who were developing a construction unit within the church. Norman Jackson advised me and helped connect me to a man to do the building, finishing, and adding to the original house.

As construction progressed, I learned my current house would be renovated for the next Bishop. What now? My next-door neighbors and good friends, Rev. Enock Rwakalembe and his pregnant wife Enid welcomed me to stay until I could move to the village. Enid was from a rural village and had great fun learning about a tape recorder and hearing her own voice. We would sit together on the steps and laugh hysterically. They had financial struggles but never made me feel that I was a bother. I ended up driving Enid to the hospital and then sitting all night with Enock waiting for the baby. They named the baby Carol which touched me deeply. Now I needed to move because my friends really needed the room.

I finally moved into the house I had built in Nsooro in 1998. The area lacked electricity and running water, but I had the house plumbed and wired for the future. Having no electricity meant no refrigerator. I learned how to shop and cook daily. Without a stove, I cooked on a kerosene one pan burner or outside with charcoal. Moses taught me that if food, especially meat or chicken, were to "sleep" overnight that it should be boiled just before we went to bed and again first thing in the morning. That kept meat safe up to two days. More than a few times my stomach told me I missed the sweet zone.

When it rained, I caught water in every container I had to avoid standing in line and having to pay at the water kiosk. When I had to buy water, nice neighbors helped me load sloshing leaden plastic jerry cans into the car. I washed clothes by hand and would only hang them when at home; otherwise, they would be stolen right off the line. I learned to appreciate water after so many years of carrying every single drop that I used. I think of the people who never have running water their whole life.

In many ways, my limited circumstances seemed appropriate. Norman and Isobel really got after me, insisting I live a bit better. They emphasized that denying myself did not help others at all. The Jacksons bought me my first refrigerator once electricity came to the village. I think I was in such shock at so much poverty and hunger and death all around that I felt guilty living well.

One day, a little female dog appeared at the house. She belonged to a witch living a couple of houses down from me. She cowered when I reached for her. I could see welts through her matted fur. One of her legs was scabbed. The woman was torturing her. I went to the witch asking to buy the dog. She refused. A week later the dog came back with barbed wire choking her. I cut off the wire, cringing myself as the little one flinched. I was determined to let her stay with me. I went to the witch's house, shoving 20,000 USh toward her, about $10 back then.

"I'm keeping your dog," I said.

"You can't take my dog," she said, glaring. "I'll put a bad hex. Evil will come."

"Madam, Jesus is stronger than your power."

The village learned that she had threatened me with her evil. People would watch me when I stopped at our small trading center for tomatoes or japaties or something. One evening several weeks later, as I was leaving the trading center, a huge storm was looming. I saw my witch with a large bag of potatoes ready to carry home. I pushed the passenger door open and called to her.

"Madam, *injura ningyi muno, togende abamuka.*" Rain very much, we go home. She lived two houses from me. The lady climbed in with a puzzled expression. The whole trading center went quiet as they watched this drama. Just as I dropped her off, the skies opened in a deluge. Two weeks later I learned she went to a local church and accepted Christ. That was wonderful! The funny/sad part is that many villagers complained that I ruined their witch. They used to go to her for remedies for physical and relationship woes. She now always has a huge smile for me when we see each other. Forgiveness is a powerful thing.

I named this little dog Lady. Rover adored her. She lived with us for about 5 years then died slowly, painfully from what I think was cancer. Where I live, we have no doctors for pets.

Rover lived to the ripe age of 16 and was by then at my house where I now live in the upper part of my hostel. I taught him to lead on a leash and not chase chickens. Our chickens are not exactly pets. We ate them as well as collected eggs. Back then, the only chickens for eating were live chickens that had to be killed. I'm relieved that our local store finally brings in dead chickens that I don't have to strangle or pluck! Rover didn't chase the animals, but he bit more than one leg while I lived in the village. He was a fearless protector.

Sometimes water and electricity were niceties and so was justice. We were afforded limited safety from the LCs – local council, a local law officer of sorts. The LCs were given minimum training. During the ADF war years, they were given guns after going through some basic training. Now, they no longer are allowed to carry guns, and citizens cannot get gun permits. Lawlessness is a huge problem with too many thieves. There is no phoning 911 for help. Often police refuse to come if they are not paid. I almost understand as most get no more than $120 a month, and police housing is nearly unlivable. They are not all corrupt, but they work at a huge disadvantage. Even when they catch a criminal, if the person has money and can't pay the police to drop the charges, they pay the judges instead. Thankfully, this kind of behavior is lessening these days with anti-corruption organizations fighting it. Some of our politicians are also against it.

During construction, a metallic door was delivered to the property. That night, someone stole it. Angry, I asked the LC in what type of neighborhood does a door get carried away when so many people are around to see it. The next day, he asked me to come with him. He led me through paths where only bicycles could travel and brought me to a mud house with a metal door. It was quite funny to see my door tied to the front opening of a mud hut with banana fibers. The LC tied the occupant's elbows together behind his back and led him about a mile to a trading center that consisted of old shops selling various things. By the time we reached the center, half of the village followed, and kids ran around playing and laughing. The adults sat down on rocks or the ground. They brought an old wooden chair out for me then started the "trial".

The thief broke loose and threw himself on the ground in front of me. He begged me to forgive him.

While I seriously considered, I noticed the congregating men picking up rocks, sticks, and other weapons. The LC ordered me to hurry to my car, while keeping the villagers from beating the thief. I drove the man to the police station where they took forever taking down information by hand, slowly finishing and having me sign the statement. They imprisoned the man for about six months.

The villagers had planned to kill the thief who we managed to get to the police. I did not know at the time that villagers beat a man to death when he is caught stealing. Often thieves steal food and goats and things the people depend on for life. The police do little, knowing the thief will soon steal again.

I saw the man's wife and several small kids at his mud house, and I felt terrible depriving them of what little he provided. Since I had a large *matooke* area, banana plants, on my property, I sent word that the wife could take any she needed. I worried about the family. About six months later, the ADF rebel group attacked the prison. They killed several guards and took prisoners to be in their army. The morning after the attack, I shared with an English-speaking neighbor how worried I was for "my thief." He laughed and told me the prison released the man two days before. I was so glad, but then I became concerned about my safety, wondering how angry he might still be with me. A few days later, he came walking by. He greeted me with a shy smile. He was grateful that I helped feed his family while he was imprisoned. He escaped ADF conscription when thousands throughout the country didn't. In his prison alone, 365 prisoners were taken out of the 627 who were there. He was very lucky.

Chapter 15

Love Through Conflict

I've mentioned the ADF a few times now. The Allied Democratic Forces were and still are a rebel group trying to disorganize the country. Many people ask me what their fight is about. I have no real answer. The war was often referred to as a "rebellion without a cause." Normal activity in this fertile part of the country abruptly halted. Crops went untended in the fields. Tens of thousands of people were forced to flee their homes to find shelter in the sprawling displaced people's camps. The unlucky ones were killed or abducted.

They are Muslim based, but I hate to mention that because of Muslim phobia, especially in the US. I do not see their fight as anything to do with religion. The rebels took in many uneducated village young people with promises of riches. They convinced recruits that the government was against them, persecuting them, preventing them from a good life. They kidnapped children as young as 10 years old to be soldiers. The ADF would get youths drunk and give them drugs. When child fighters tried to escape from the rebel base in the mountains, fellow students were forced to kill them. They were all circumcised and given Muslim names and daily brain washing. Drugged and servile, the rebels made these boys kill other children or elderly until the young men believed they could never join normal society again.

When you live through war, life goes on. You eat breakfast, brush your teeth, etc., etc. You get used to the 8 p.m. curfew, hold your visits to the latrine until daylight, and never go anywhere after dark. Everyone spoke of daily attacks and horrors, yet things seemed OK. I had a *mzungu* friend close to delivering her baby, and I held a baby shower for her. The night before the shower, the rebels attacked the prison and took about 300 prisoners for their cause. The family lived close to the prison and spent the night on the floor below windows to avoid gunshots. We had the party, but the family left that same afternoon.

I did wonder where to head if we had an attack. Kabarole Hill is next to a girl's boarding school. Rebels would attack such schools for the men to have women. The side lawn of the diocese had an old tree with a huge hollowed out hole in the trunk. I easily fit inside, so I had my escape plan. However, I never spent a night in it. Fort Portal had quite a large army protecting the town and escaped many attacks. My friend Rev. Ezra lived about 25 kilometers away where things were much worse. He and his family and several neighbors slept in the bush at night with different men taking watch. I gave them as many blankets and tarps as I was able to get because sleeping in the rain is hard.

I sometimes visited a local shop, Andrew's and Brothers, to buy goods and maybe stop for a visit. Andrew Amooti Kaliba and his wife Jolly Abwooli Kaliba ran the small shop on a back street. Andrew and Jolly befriended me when I first arrived in Fort Portal. Back then, they asked my advice on what *bzungu* enjoyed or what I missed being so far from my country.

"Why?" I asked. I was almost the only *mzungu* around then. "I miss chocolate, potato chips, ice cream and buying dead chicken." That got me a look until I explained I meant, already slaughtered and cleaned poultry. They now have all of that plus a whole lot more to supply the swarms of *bzungu*. Andrew has the best-known shop now on the main street of town, a restaurant called The Gardens, a hardware shop and a tourist center. Back when I didn't have much money, Andrew would sometimes hand me something extra when I bought things. He would let me run on credit when money was gone. Jolly always searched me out at a group or party. I am sort of awkward and shy in social settings, and she is the same. They both have been supportive and friendly from the first when I truly needed that friendship.

I remember sitting in front of Andrew's, enjoying a Coke and watching many *bzungu* families packed and leaving the area when two American men came up to me.

"Madame, you must evacuate," they said.

"And who are you?" I asked.

"The US embassy, Madame. Ms. Adams, you must leave Fort Portal."

"I will not," I said. "I've recently returned from the US and prefer it here."

"Do you not see the helicopters? The hummers? Tanks could pass through any time."

"They've nothing to do with me," I said.

"They're fighting a war, protecting you."

"I hope they do their jobs well because I'm not leaving."

"This war is not for *bzungu*, foolish people like you. The soldiers don't have time to worry about reckless foreigners. If you refuse to come with us, then we no longer are responsible for you."

"Nevertheless, I won't leave," I said, finishing my Coke more casually than I felt. Fort Portal was now my home, and I wasn't leaving.

The men were right about the soldiers, a crude and often scary lot. Many were rough, and a couple of my girls were raped.

Yet, good exists as well. I was on my front lawn when I saw a fully armed soldier walking past. He looked like a kid. He was so cute.

"Hello," I said, which surprised him. He stopped and glanced at me cautiously. Most people feared soldiers.

"Thank you for being here and making me feel

safer."

I saw him lift his chin and straighten his shoulders. He almost grew a foot.

"I'm here for you," he said, pride in his voice and posture. While he was stationed here, he often stopped in to make sure I was OK. Even through evil and chaos, love and peace can also exist.

Fort Portal needed the donation container I had filled in Hawaii and California. It kept being detained here and there. Getting tax clearance proved a challenge, requiring me to go to Kampala. On one of the trips, I traveled with Bishop Eustace, another Ugandan man and Charles the driver. On returning, torrential rains made the regular road impassable. We took the long route—2 sides of a triangle that ended up in Fort Portal on tarmac roads. Leaving Kampala, we got a flat tire, keeping us out way too late on the road. We crossed the equator just before dark only to be stopped by the army about a half mile beyond. Dressed in full combat gear, they warned us of rebels fighting up ahead. The bishop wanted to head back to the nearest town and find lodgings, but the army commander prevented us, insisting we spend the night in the car there by the disorganized army camp.

When they realized a bishop and a *mzungu* lady sat in the car, the commander gave us a small hut for the night. The small round shelter held no furnishing of any kind, and it smelled strongly of fish. As exhausted and hungry as we were, we sat around on the floor joking about poor room service in our "hotel." As we were talking, the commander came in with some stale, dry bread and some warm drinking water for us to share. We laughed even harder.

Our sleeping arrangements resembled a cartoon. I ended up against the far wall from the doorway (no actual door), while the bishop, Charles, and the other man lay with their feet towards the opening. Charles, who could have taken the entire hut by himself, lay by my middle, and his feet hung out the hut. In the terrible heat, mosquitoes swarmed. I shared some mosquito repellent, so now the hut smelled of fish and bug spray. In the distance, we heard gunfire and bomb explosions.

Charles started a prayer: "Oh Lord, we know you are our protector. We pray for protection from those bombs that the enemy sends from those big guns. Lord, please let them not come close enough to land on us. Lord we also pray for safety with the army men who are all around us and very undisciplined. And lastly, Lord please protect us from the big poison snakes that might come into this hut in the night. In Jesus name we pray. Amen."

Amen and the three men were asleep in no time while I lay wide awake. I hadn't given bombs, unfriendly soldiers, and snakes a thought before the prayer.

Sometime in the night, I badly needed a short call – toilet break. I tried to move quietly, but Charles got up and followed me at a distance for protection. I saw no latrines, so I walked out from the camp a short distance. When I felt my foot hit something round and hard, I froze in fear. Did landmines protect the camp? I didn't dare move but when nothing happened, I squatted right there and emptied my bladder. In the morning I found that I had peed in a pumpkin patch.

Daily life went on, less scary than some might think. One learns to live in one's circumstances.

While running Child Care Outreach, I met a German man – Stefan Kluge – and his Ugandan wife Mariam. Stefan had three horses, given to him by some *mzungu* missionaries who were running away from the war. I introduced myself and convinced them to allow me to teach riding at their farm.

Practicing with the horses connected me to my former life. No matter where you are in the world, horses remain the same – sometimes gentle, sometimes spirited. They smell of sweat and leather. They have a language in whinnies I understand, much like a mother understands the meaning of a baby's cry. Running my hands through their manes, enticing them to a gallop, seeing their response at having a task, brings me great joy. What prepared me to work with children in a foreign country with a seemingly insurmountable language barrier? I'm thankful for magnificent creatures which helped build my skill, patience and perseverance and my time working with students at Mauka Lani Stables.

Mariam and Stefan became fast friends. By then, I had left the church house and moved to my small house in Nsooro. The Kluges worried about me living alone. They also realized I was often hungry. They regularly drove over to make sure I was ok and invited me over for a shower (remember, my village lacked running water). The thought of Miriam's cooking made my stomach grumble (then and now). Stefan being German and a great chef himself, they cooked wonderful *bzungu* food that I didn't get anyplace else. I really missed foods that I couldn't get easily. They would check on me after nearby rebel attacks. Mariam Kluge is now treasurer of my NGO Board of Directors, and we continue to be close to this day. Back in the war years, I really needed that friendship!

The horse training lasted less than a year. I didn't get much teaching business as most locals have little money for recreation and most *bzungu* ran away from the war. That brief time with the horses and the love I felt from new, true friends are some of my happiest memories, even as the rebel situation saddened those of us who stayed.

In June 1998, ADF rebels attacked a vocational school in Kichwamba, a town near us. Over 100 kids burned to death while many others were taken for child soldiers. Many parents to this day do not know if their child died in the fire or at the hands of a soldier.

Several of Moses' friends were killed in the school attack. Two managed to escape. The stories they told were horrendous. I do not think those young men will ever be normal after the experience.

The church held a service for everyone who lost a child or family member as well as the public. My heart broke to hear the mothers wailing and to see everyone in tears. Near the end of the service, the Bishop asked us to pray for the rebels that God would touch and forgive them.

Angered as I'd been with the priest at Edwin's death, I ran out of the church. My dear friend Rev. Enock (whose baby was named after me), followed me out.

"*Adyeeri*, stop," he called. "Are you ok?"

"I cannot forgive the rebels," I cried. "I will NOT forgive them. I hate them."

"Come sit with me," Enock said, leading me under a tree.

"I don't understand how they can do these horrors," I said.

"How many rebels have you met?" he asked.

"None, of course," I answered.

"Then you have no one to hate," he replied.

"I hate the people killing our babies," I hiccupped my anguish.

"You hate their acts. I do, too. We hate the acts, not a particular person," he said.

"Why not?" I said, determined in my tears.

"God loves all people," he said. "Through our prayers, He can touch hearts."

These misled, uneducated young people now find themselves in such horrendous situations and do not know how to get out.

Enock's words are a good lesson for many situations.

I admit that I kept hating the rebels but grew more aware of the complexities. Many rebels were uneducated and brainwashed young villagers. Others wanted to back out of the horrific situations they found themselves in but were stuck. I still feel the leaders of such horror are pure evil.

With the war raging, the impact of Child Care Outreach increased daily. In my second year in Uganda, I partnered with Send a Cow UK to assist families with goat and chicken projects. From the funds I raised, we helped build more than ten local homes. I had water catchment tanks added to many homes; I had fuel saving brick and mud cooking stoves built. Overall, I kept busy building up families and sending more and more kids to school despite the dangers.

Once on the way to town, I saw four young men with their heads blown through, dead on the side of the road. They had their hands tied behind their backs. I think they were killed by local militia rather than rebels. Giving out guns to scared, poorly trained people is NOT a good idea.

When I moved to Nsooro, my LC lived across the street from me. I was more afraid of him with a gun than of a possible rebel attack. One night I heard gunshots. The next morning, I learned the LC shot out his window when he heard something moving. He protected us from a goat. Better a dead goat than a dead child.

The same LC came to me when I first moved into the house.

"Madame, your rubbish burn pit is too small," he said. "For a few shillings, my son will dig a proper size hole."

"What's the right size?" I asked.

"It must be at least a meter deep," he said.

"Sorry," I smiled, "we Americans don't use metric. Why don't we cross over to your house, and you can show me the correct size?"

"No need, my son knows," he said.

"I'd like to see for myself. I assume yours is right."

He grumbled something and walked off, trying again a few days later.

"Madame, your *matooke* is too messy. Rebels can hide there."

I looked at my *matooke* and then pointedly looked across the street to his. This time I didn't even have to say anything. He didn't bother me much after that.

During the ADF war period, in 1999, I met a young German woman, Carolyn Vom Stein, and we became fast friends. She volunteered with the infants' home in town. We often traveled together. We delivered food to child-headed families and investigated conditions. We enjoyed Easter at a crater lake. A fifth of Uganda is covered in lakes and rivers, including Lake Victoria, the third largest in the world. We enjoyed sharing a coke as we sat in front of Andrew's shop. There were few *bzungu* around in those days. Carolyn's friendship continued even after she went home. I visited her and her family in Germany. I gave my first presentation of my program in a German church. By the time I went to her wedding, I had developed friendships and support from several churches in her area.

In those years, I took several trips outside of the country. I needed time away from the fighting and fear. I enjoyed hot showers, good food and electricity. While I felt I had adjusted well, I still wasn't completely at home with rustic living either for myself or those around me.

One time I heard one of my kids who lived up in the mountains was seriously ill. Rev. Ezra agreed to visit him with me. We headed out in my old car, no 4-wheel drive, making our way up the mountain along bicycle paths. Fortunately, the child was less ill than reported. Heading back down the mountain, the engine quit. I thought maybe it wasn't getting enough gas. I tried to clean out the glass gas thing and tube that connected the carburetor. I asked Ezra to try starting the car as I stood beside it. I forgot he did not know how to drive. He turned the key without stepping on the clutch. The car leaped over my feet – thank God it was muddy – and stalled. We got it running, but if I slowed down at all, it would stall. As darkness approached, we worried rebels could be anywhere. We headed down the bike paths leaning on the horn while ladies with their heads piled high with produce and kids all leaped aside into the bushes for safety as we flew by completely out of control. We were both scared but laughing like a pair of fools. We reached a bridge made of parallel logs with wide gaps. We had no choice but to fly over it as well. We managed to get off the mountain and make it home in a coughing car that died in the driveway. The next day, my mechanic told me that it was not possible to have driven that car. But we did!!!!!

We laughed when we could, with the war only peripherally intruding.

At Kabarole Hill, I had my escape tree. In my house I had a more prosaic attic. A wooden hatch opened to the attic with a rope ladder that could be pulled in. I lived alone when Moses was in boarding school. One late night, I heard a banging on my bedroom window. My handicapped neighbor who always cared about me but spoke no English kept saying ADF in a panicked voice. Under the full moon, as I looked out my window, I saw many neighbors running down the road. I told the man to go. Rather than follow, I went up my rope ladder to hide in the attic. I was afraid that my white skin would stand out and catch the attention of the rebels. I slept the rest of the night on a mattress I kept up there. The rebels never got as far as our village that night. The next morning, I headed back to the office as usual.

One thing I will never forget is how horrible a displacement camp is. Uganda's economy is predominantly agriculture. The soils are fertile with small farms dotting the hillsides. Ugandan coffee, tea, cotton, and tobacco are the main exports, and farms support families with cassava (manioc, tapioca), potatoes, corn, millet and matooke. The limited protein comes from beans. Wealthier families have cows, goats, and chickens raised on the family farm. When the fighting became the most violent, tens of thousands of farmers and their families fled the land, often leaving the crops to rot or turn wild. Over a hundred thousand people filled camps around Bundibugyo, in the mountains west of Fort Portal.

Each day, public convoys, protected by the Ugandan army driving "Black Mamba" armored personnel carriers, brought in food and supplies. Ironic, given so many in the camps were farmers, with crops still in the field and livestock left to the rebels. I traveled to one camp with the Catholic Relief Services. They were bringing in food, and I brought clothes and blankets from our container. Thousands of people lived in grass shacks on top of each other. They had little food and no sanitation. The smells and hopeless faces will live with me forever. Even in squalor, life continues. I was handed a newborn baby to hold. I later learned the mother hoped I would take the baby with me, knowing her chances of survival were small.

When food was brought out, the camp section leaders were supposed to gather enough for a certain number of people. Instead, the desperate people started fighting and screaming. Soldiers fired into the air and locked away the food. An old woman fell at my feet begging me to get her food. Kids scrambled for spilled flour in the dirt and licked it off their hands. They grabbed uncooked beans and ate them. The scene was heartbreaking, and there was nothing I could do. That night I felt sick eating my supper.

I used to feel guilty eating good food and having warm blankets and a dry bed. My friends the Jacksons told me over and over that I needed to take care of myself to be able to do any good – a hard lesson to learn amid such need.

I worked as hard during the war as I do now. I wasn't cowering for my life. I really need to be clear because I certainly never want to come off like the «Machine Gun Preacher,» a writer who claims heroic acts in another rebel situation. The book and movie about Sam Childers and his efforts are so exaggerated that the people of South Sudan are furious. He established an orphanage in that war torn country, but the stories of rescue are nothing short of miracles. He's been investigated by the FBI and IRS. The faction he fought with have distanced themselves, and some question his forceful taking of children to the orphanage as a form of bullying itself. Reports say he has not visited the orphanage in years, and the situation has devolved to where the kids have inadequate care and poor food. I have had several people tell me," Oh, you are like the machine gun preacher." No way!!!! I wonder how he got the Mother Theresa peace award while shooting people.

The closest I came to being part of the war came when I visited one of my kids who had cholera. To get to him, I drove alone on a path through a field of tall elephant grass. As I reached the other side, four men stepped out with automatic guns aimed at my head. I hit the brake and stalled the car.

"*Mzungu*, what are you doing here?" one asked.

I sat frozen.

They all started laughing, nudging each other and pointing at my face.

"We are protecting this village. You shouldn't be here." They were local armed village security who heard my car coming where cars did not usually travel.

"Don't drive around here. The rebels will get you," they said, laughter fading.

I did go another couple kilometers to pick up the child and bring him to care but was sort of scared to go so far alone again.

Those of us who stayed, cared for each other more than we cared about some possible attack. During this time, I spent Christmas ill in the hospital. Almost all the clergy from the

Cathedral visited with their wives and prayed with me. I was deeply touched that they would come on such a day to check on me. They wanted to make sure I had bedding and food. At hospitals then, your daily care came from family and friends.

We continued our outreach to the huge number of OVC -- orphaned and vulnerable children. We heard gunshots and mortar blasts. We took cover, just in case. We lived with the same underlying fear so many endure where guns and violence are ubiquitous. I never took up arms myself, though I did cradle children in my arms. I didn't join a faction for protection or vengeance, but I did pray for peace and forgiveness. Mostly, I took in kids, raised funds for their care, and stayed when so many others left.

Chapter 16

Death and a
Sense of Humor

Sometimes I feel if there is a commotion to be found, I'll find it.

During the 2006 elections for Ugandan president, riots broke out in Kampala. I had to take one of my charges with a severe heart condition, Peter, to the city hospital. I was hit by tear gas when my taxi was caught in the riot. Even with a cloth over my face, inhaling the tear gas burned my lungs, making me cough until I thought I'd vomit. It burned my eyes and my skin. Drool and snot are not pretty. I swore that I would stay away from any large crowds from then on.

I returned to the city the next week with Rwakojo Grace, my field officer. We headed to Mengo, a quiet friendly place a bit out of the city – to be safer. I insisted on staying in a small out-of-the-way guest house. After visiting Peter, I ventured into the city to buy several things unavailable in Fort Portal. I made my way back to the guest house sitting sideways on a *boda* – it is considered wrong for a lady to sit astride, plus with a skirt, it is hard. I was holding a dozen packages. As we reached Mengo, near the Bugandan King's headquarters, I noticed a restless crowd in front of us. My *boda* driver also realized things were bad. Just as we came to a junction where we would turn right, we heard a huge racket. I thought a truck was having major engine problems, but as we got a bit closer, we saw people running or throwing tables and barrels and things into the road. The truck was not backfiring. It was burning. My driver careened on to a bumpy, dirt shortcut where many were already racing to get away. I heard bangs and yelled, "is that gunfire?" But the *boda* man was too intent on running away to answer my question. I was sitting so that I could see what was happening behind us as the driver sped forward down the dirt, single-track. On another *boda*, I saw another passenger's face blown off. The boda kept racing with the man hanging on, blood gushing from his head. The poor man lived but with a terrible wounded face and eye. By then, the whole street was filled with hundreds of running people and *bodas* and screaming and total chaos.

Now this sounds crazy, but we were ravenous, and the guest house didn't serve food. The area we had barely escaped had the only restaurants nearby. We did not know the size of the riot, but we braved the streets near the Mengo junction. We walked carefully, out of range of the shooting. We were about a block from the major action, and all the shops and restaurants had their doors locked. Cracking open a closed door, one owner motioned for us to come. We raced across the road, and they quickly let us in and locked the doors. The scene was surreal. As I ate a nice chicken dinner, I watched soldiers set up machine guns on tripods. Huge *mumbas*, the armored vehicles, passed with guns sticking out the top. Meanwhile, school kids headed home, walking in and out of the broken glass, around the police barrier, burned truck and guns. Others stood in groups near doorways in case they had to hurriedly retreat. Through the fear and the blood and the kindness of the restaurant owner, the memory I carry most clearly from that day is my *boda* driver taking crazy turns and yelling to me, "hang hard, Mama!!!" as we careened through the bushes trying to escape the riot.

Safely home in Fort Portal, I went to Sunday service at the Cathedral the next day. During prayers, congregants can go forward to give thanks. I stepped to the altar grateful for surviving the Mengo riot. When I returned to my seat, I found my bag opened and my wallet, filled with funds from my trip, was gone. The lady behind us said the man sitting beside me had taken the wallet. The thief was found the next day knocked out drunk. Almost a week later my wallet, minus the 1,100,000 Ush cash, was found with my driver permit and even a credit card still in it. The lady who saw the thief volunteered to speak at the trial. After the woman gave her testimony, the judge asked the thief if he had any questions.

"Yes," he replied. "I want to know why the witness did not close her eyes during the prayer time. She should not have been watching as I took madam's wallet."

The lady judge, while trying not to laugh, pounded her gavel and said, "confession of crime noted, sentence to be set Tuesday next week."

As I often say, you have to have a sense of humor.

In June 2001, I received a message that my sister Jean was alone in a hospital in Wasilla, Alaska. My brother Henry had a vacation trip planned with his wife and said he couldn't get there. I took on the long trip. Jean's friend, Johnnie, picked me up at the airport. In June, the sun shines almost 23 hours a day in Alaska. I longed for a bit of sleep before seeing Jean in the hospital. Johnnie thoughtfully set up a spare bedroom with black curtains. At the hospital the next morning, I found Jean in an alarming condition. She hallucinated much of the time but at least recognized me. Half the time she thought she was a small girl and at other times she thought the nursing staff plotted to kill her. She had terminal cancer and severe dementia. The doctors recommended hospice care. I spent the following days looking at different hospice homes and settling Jean's affairs and bills. Johnnie loaned me a bicycle to go back and forth to the hospital. I stayed for about 10 days.

Saying goodbye on the last day, I knew that it was the last time I would see Jean on earth. I tried to share the love of God with her, but Jean refused to listen.

"Remember," I told her before leaving, "if you ever

become scared, all you have to do is call on Jesus."

On her last day alive, Jean became agitated and kept screaming that evil people were in her room. The caregiver reminded her of my parting words. Shortly after, Jean called out asking Jesus to save her. Jean smiled and told her "My sister was right." She saw angels sitting at the foot of the bed. She told the caregiver that Jesus hugged her. Her caregiver wrote me a letter weeks after to tell me. Jean died on Thanksgiving Day 2001.

On January 2, 2003, I learned my brother Bill had died with no one to handle the burial or manage his affairs. I always loved Bill dearly, and the news was shocking.

"Hi Henry," I said, phoning my other brother from Fort Portal. "Bill has died. I am told that he was virtually alone, and there is no one to settle his affairs."

"Oh, I am sorry to hear, but you know we were never close." He replied.

"I do know that, but things need to be settled for his burial and to settle any of his affairs. Could you fly down to Alabama?"

"I am busy. The state will handle him as an indigenous person. I see no reason to go there. Like I said, I'm busy here." Henry is strictly unemotional about everything in his life.

"Looks like I need to go," I said, ending the call.

I spoke with Henry in the morning, my time. By 10 a.m., I was on the phone to a travel company. They booked me on a 9 pm flight. I needed seven hours to get to the airport, with a stop at the travel agency for the tickets. I threw some clothes in a suitcase, and my friend Sandra who was staying with me, sped us off to the airport. We cut things so close, I couldn't even stop at the currency exchange shop for US dollars. When I picked up the tickets, the travel agency phoned the airport that I was on the way, to allow me through. We raced to the airport. I rushed through the inspections and boarded just as the gate was closing.

From there, I caught my breath on the long, long flights to Amsterdam and then NYC. I arrived in Montgomery, Alabama the next evening. There I realized that I did not have a dime on me. I went to withdraw money with a credit card only to find I'd forgotten my pin number. I was exhausted from traveling and lack of sleep, and close to tears.

"Honey, you look really upset," a middle-aged lady said in a heavy Southern accent.

That close to finished me, but I managed to quaver out the whole story. She and her husband took me to eat and drove me to a hotel which accepted my card, and I collapsed for the night. No one can tell me that God does not put guardian angels in my path when I need them the most.

The next days were a miserable blur. When I went for Bill's body at the state morgue, I encountered a lot of red tape and confusion involving trying to find his "misplaced" body. I also changed hotels because I couldn't afford to keep paying so much. The step down was somewhat drastic to a bit of a dump. I remember being constantly chilled. Alabama is cold in January, and I had packed my normal, hot weather clothes.

I met Bill's friend Tommy who had been taking care of him, living with Bill in a dilapidated old Southern mansion that Bill owned. Bill was never what I would call neat, but he died in the most horrible squalor that I could imagine. I had hoped to stay in his house and save hotel charges, but the house was uninhabitable. I also found Bill's huge dog who had been Bill's close companion. He was so confused and upset. After some investigations, I found that Bill held clear title to the house. I asked Tommy if he wanted it signed over to him, the only catch was that he had to continue caring for the dog. Tommy acted as if I offered him a fortune.

I arranged for Bill's burial in a pauper's graveyard. The cemetery was unkempt and joyless, but I knew it would not have mattered to Bill. And I simply could not find an affordable grave site on such short notice. Bill's boss from work, myself, and Tommy were the only ones at the funeral. With Tommy driving me, I found an affordable lawyer to turn over the property to him. With the stress and weather, I became so ill that Tommy took me to an emergency room. The hospital treated me horribly because I had no insurance and little money. The staff sent me away even though I had a high fever, and some sort of a bad flu was hitting people. I managed to continue with the legal work. Bill left behind two ex-wives and several kids. We didn't know who they were except for his first-born son Dylan. He left me free to do whatever I wanted with the house and property. Bill's boss called me and asked me to meet him at the office of his computer company where Bill worked. As it turned out, Bill had left a huge insurance policy in my name alone. The money would go a long way in my work in Uganda. I was shocked! I had no idea at the time the ripple effect that Bill's generosity would have. It's amazing how much impact you can have when you share your blessings.

I had been talking with a friend Jeannie in Iowa by phone who realized I was terribly sick. She phoned my brother Henry and told him to get himself down to Alabama. Jeannie was always direct. Henry arrived during my last days there, and I did really appreciate that he cared enough about me to fly down as I was so very sick. He saw Bill's house and was not too upset about me giving it to Tommy. When Henry drove me to the airport, I could tell he was hurt that I did not share the insurance funds. I felt my kids in Uganda and I needed the money more than Henry. He had a family, a doctorate in meteorology, and had retired from the Air Force as a colonel.

Of all my trips to the US, this was the hardest. I arrived back to Uganda still suffering from the horrible flu. Things were busy at the program. Sandra was helping and really wanted me to get back, but I spent five days with my friends the Jacksons in the Jinja area resting and healing before heading back to Fort Portal.

Chapter 17

Impact and Many Hats

I spent much time in prayer about the best way to use the money I inherited from Bill. I decided to keep it in my private account, rather than the Child Care Outreach account with the church while I waited for clarity from the Lord. Of course, different people had ideas for the money, but I felt I needed to use it on some sort of income generating project so it could continue working and supporting the program rather than a one-time expense.

My reach and my children were growing. Through various activities, I've helped over 2000 students escape the trials of their childhood. Chris Ategeka was yet another kid who needed help with school. He arrived scrawny and barefoot, highly recommended by a friend of mine. He was being raised by a deaf grandmother and eager to learn. He was and is creative, with a poet's spirit. If he has one idea, he has a dozen. I first put him in a local secondary school. As he continued and did well, I brought him to town and sent him to a better school where he excelled.

He was sponsored by Martha and Mike Helms and their family in California. We require the students to write thank you letters to their sponsors. I helped Chris write more than the obligatory thank you. We provided paper, helped with English, encouraged expression. He might not agree, but like so many others of my teens, he gave me quite a bit of trouble. And, like so many, mostly he was a good kid. He'd bend over the blank sheet, eager to share what he learned that day and to tell me that someday he'd be rich and famous and do great deeds for his family – meaning all of us in Fort Portal and even Uganda.

The Helms decided to help Chris get into college in the US. As he grew up and when he was in California, he continued to keep in touch with me. That makes me feel so, so good. He has grown into a caring man who I have grown to love as a son. When I had neck surgery, he drove from San Francisco to Los Angeles to show up and surprise me in my hospital room. He loves to show up at my door here in Uganda without letting me know he is coming. He regales others about my work and my fame, exaggerated, I'm sure. I am just doing what I can in a very small part of a huge, troubled world. This book is largely due to Chris' insistence, assistance and encouragement.

With children like Chris to care for, I committed

to using my brother's generosity on a program which would continue to generate income. After much prayer, I decided to build a hostel for travelers on a budget. I began searching for land in an inviting and accessible location. I visited many places, and my community knew I was looking. I received a phone call from a man willing to sell me an ideal plot in Boma, about one mile outside Fort Portal. He offered a generous price because he admired the work I was doing. I bought the land, then consulted Norman Jackson who was running the Rwenzori Construction Company at the Church of Uganda. We discussed what we could build with the available funds. I had a small parcel, so I wanted a storied building. Norman said I did not have enough money, so I told him to design the structure in such a way that I could continue building once I found more funds. He thought that I was being foolish but went along with it anyway.

Sometimes I am more foolish than others. A man came to the office at the hostel asking to borrow a wheelbarrow he said he needed to work with my neighbors. I believed him and let it go. Instead of going to the neighbor, he raced down the road and grabbed a *boda* and took off. Some neighbors grabbed another *boda* and caught him. By the time they came back, about twenty men had gathered. The thief broke away and ran to the office begging me to "save him." I asked David, an employee at the hostel, to get the police while staving off the men screaming, demanding the thief.

"I'm not letting you kill this man over a wheelbarrow,"

I said.

"No worries, Adyeeri," they said. "We'll kill him down the road, not in front of you."

Fortunately, the police came and took the man which made the neighbors angry with me. I gave the leaders of the gang some money and thanked them for catching the thief. We all had a chance to cool down. Later that day, the police came for a full report. They wanted my wheelbarrow for evidence. I refused to let them have it. They told me that if I wanted the thief sentenced, I needed to give them money. "Forget it. Let him go," I said. He certainly would stay clear of my neighbors, and I get tired of police asking for money.

As I see it, there are a couple of reasons behind mob justice. The biggest one is the complete lack of justice and the large number of thieves. Unemployment is rampant and uneducated youth are hanging out with no jobs. Stealing is an insidious problem, and people are sick of it. When someone is caught, a large group quickly forms and somehow people who would never do certain things join in with high emotions and anger. I have some orphans in my program whose dad was killed by a mob for theft and later they found out it was the wrong man.

In some cases, I almost understand. Libya's leader Qaddafi was the friend of Queen Best Kemigisa, the Queen Mother of our region. When he would come to Fort Portal, the traffic and commotion were crazy. I saw him several times and had to chuckle about his guards – all women in full guard uniform. When Qaddafi built a palace for our king, the gossip was that he would give good money for five baby's heads to bury in the foundation. A man got very drunk and in broad daylight he grabbed a baby at our trading center and with a *panga* (a type of machete), he cut off her head. I was driving home from town and saw a mob of angry people and a beheaded baby on the side of the road. The mob killed the man, and I stayed completely out of that situation. That one seemed justified to me.

As I continued running the program under the Church of Uganda, back in the US, a gay bishop was ordained in New Hampshire. The decision raised a huge ruckus in the Anglican church here. The Ugandan Anglican church severed all ties with US Episcopal churches. This added extra tension to conflicts I was already having with Bishop Benezeri Kisembo of the Rwenzori Diocese. He already did not approve of many of my expenditures and projects. He also felt I should reach out to all the people in the diocese. To run such a vast area correctly would take an immense amount of travel. I believed better to focus my impact rather than dilute my efforts.

The breaking point came during a meeting of diocesan priests and workers. The bishop called for elections of a new board to run the Child Care Outreach program. I requested that the current board be kept. "Sit down and be quiet." He told me. I then was ordered to return any "sinful" American money back to the sender. After the meeting, I met with the bishop in his office.

"I can't and I won't return the money," I said.

"I have decided, and I'm in charge," he replied.

"That money is for school fees and to meet the needs of the kids," I argued.

"It is sinful money," he said.

"Money isn't sinful. It's how you use it that's sinful," I said.

"You use it incorrectly, against my wishes. I know you're channeling funds to help Catholic children."

No turning back now, the conversation escalated.

"I don't care what religion a suffering kid was born into. I will help those who God led me to find---PERIOD!"

"This is God's house. We must care for our own. We must repudiate sin and all that emanates from sin."

"You're going to make the kids suffer because of some theological difference?"

"When two elephants fight, the grass suffers," he said.

"Your excellency's elephants will always fight," I said.

That did NOT go over well.

"I've had enough of your disrespect," he raised his voice.

"Then act like a wise and loving leader," I countered. Not like a bigoted idiot, I thought, but responded, "I think I need to transplant my grass."

"Leave," he ordered, "but the car, motorcycles, everything, belongs to the Church. They stay."

"What?! I bought the car with my own money. I brought in the funds and donations for everything I use, everything I'm going to keep using."

"They stay," he said with finality.

"If you're going to be a thief and steal my things – you, not the Church – there's nothing I can do about it."

"You are correct." I felt the unstated bias toward me as merely a *mzungu* woman, but even in a heated argument, that would have gone beyond the ingrained rules of Ugandan politeness.

"I've been caring for our children, despite your prejudice. I'm continuing this work – with my things," I yelled, backing to the door.

As I opened it, several priests almost fell inside the office. I pushed past them. I headed to my office but was so upset I asked Rose Katwesige, who I'd practically adopted years before, to finish the day and close up. I did not want to break down in front of anyone, even her. I was so, so upset that the Jackson's, my wonderful friends, invited me to spend the night. We talked and prayed. The fateful meeting occurred on Friday. On Monday, I presented my resignation.

I resigned from Child Care Outreach in November. The bishop requested that I continue until the end of the year. True to his angry words, he insisted the car, the motorcycles and computers, all the things I'd bought for the program, belonged to the church. I had bought the car with my own money, in my name, so that was mine outright. The other things I feared I'd have to give up.

The other priests and the staff stepped in on my behalf. They knew I was continuing the work. Same impact – different name. They rallied around me, offering support, love and understanding. So many of us worked side by side to care for the neediest among us, bound by our mutual respect, love for the Ugandan people, and commitment to each other.

The bishop relented. I withdrew most of the Child Care Outreach money. The older students who had proven themselves and the long-term students opened bank accounts where I deposited enough funds for them to finish their secondary terms. I left about 900,000 USh in the Child Care Outreach account as well as some furniture. I photocopied bank statements and expenditure documents and all papers I would need in case of an audit.

I decided to form my own NGO. I had lived here long enough to manage the daunting task. I had friends help me write a constitution and register the application. I choose board members who were well known and respected in the area. Youth Encouragement Services (YES!) was approved in early 2005.

"Learn to do right; seek justice. Defend the oppressed. Take up the cause of the fatherless; plead the case of the widow." (Isaiah 1:17)

YES's mission is to improve the welfare of orphaned and vulnerable youth, including children born HIV positive. We help those who have no one able to care for them. We primarily invest in education for those who cannot afford to go to school. Our scholarship program sponsors around 300 orphans and vulnerable children.

We focus on education (and the needs surrounding it – food, clothing, supplies) as the best means of equipping the children we serve for meaningful work and as the best way to honor their dignity. Additionally, we respect and consider local culture within our work. YES provides orphaned and other vulnerable youth in Fort Portal with opportunities and support to become self-reliant and able to give back to their community. Every child should have the chance to become a healthy, educated, and empowered individual. With nearly half of the population of Uganda under the age of 15, the youth are truly Uganda's future.

While we are well established now, in the beginning, I had to rent an office until the Boma property for the hostel was ready. Our rented office was terrible. It was right beside the Mpanga market, our main market. I often suffered with jiggers, a sand flea that burrows into your skin. The noise and commotion were distracting. To escape, I moved the office into the lower rooms of the hostel in March of 2005 while construction continued. Finally, with some substantial donations, the building was finished.

Every child's story is mixed with sorrow and joy. A 15-year-old girl came to us desperate for school fees. She came from Rubisengo, a community over the mountain where people sell their daughters into marriage. Her father allowed her to complete primary school but sold her right after she finished. She was courageous. She heard that the law protected her. Her own mother and aunts accepted the practice and thought she was being a stubborn girl. She saved enough money to come to Fort Portal, to a human rights organization. Together, they traveled back to Rubisengo and talked with the father, who has many wives and many children. The father promised not to sell that particular daughter. She rightly lived in fear that the HIV+ man would pursue her. The girl was captured from her own father's house, tied up and thrown into the back of a pickup truck. She screamed and kicked and fought the whole time. She screamed at every area with people around. Some friends managed to get a phone call through to the human rights group. The next morning, the police came demanding the girl's location. The father admitted he'd let the man in and told them where she might be held. She was found tied and thrown on the floor of a small mud hut. The "husband" had not reached her yet to consummate, by rape, the arrangement. The police brought her to Fort Portal, and a kind lady took her in. Her father most likely kept the cows and cash he got for her, but the "husband" knew in Fort Portal he would be arrested if he tried to kidnap an underage girl.

Normally, if one can say there is ever normal, YES policy states that we assist orphans with school fees, but we chose to help this brave girl who wanted a better life. We found a sponsor to adopt her and help with her fees. Later, we sent her to nursing school. Sadly, this story isn't unusual here, and I've grown a bit desensitized to it.

About the same time I started YES and was building the hostel, a generous donation from an incredibly supportive friend, Rachel Tracey, and her family helped me build an orphanage for kids suffering from AIDS. Early on, I knew little about this disease. As I lived in the village, I started seeing it firsthand. I remember Florence, an 11-year-old girl from the neighborhood, as she came pounding at my door at 6 a.m. and threw herself in my arms crying, saying her mom was dead. I had watched Margaret as she became weaker by the day. I never expected her to make it from one day to the next as she was walking bones. The locals call the disease "slim." She died in bed where Florence found her. Antiretroviral (ARV) drugs were only starting to be known then and were out-of-reach expensive for most. The epidemic became so ubiquitous that the government started providing ARV for free, too late for Margaret. I started recognizing when someone was positive with AIDS. They had a cough, fatigue, rapid weight loss, blotches on the skin. About 70% of my children are orphaned because of AIDS. In visits to villages and local homes, I started finding sick kids who were being completely neglected. The villagers were waiting for them to die. Amidst this need, I felt compelled to build a rescue home and help these thrown away kids. Death is so common here. If it is not AIDS, it is cancer, TB, cholera, or high blood pressure. I know people who have died from an asthma attack or even ever-present malaria.

With the donation in hand, I again started searching for land. After looking at many different places, the thought came to me that perhaps I could make an apartment on an upper level of the hostel and donate my Kasusu land for the orphanage.

Norman Jackson worried I would be at my workplace day and night. I felt it would be a good move. Unfortunately, I did not have the money to finish the upper level of the hostel. The Peace Corp donated a good amount to finish part of the upper area. When the Irish donors learned of my plan, they donated enough to finish my apartment. In July 2005, I moved in.

Flowers of every color grow on this land. Sweet smells permeate the verdant green. We have fields of cows, and goats are everywhere. Uganda has hugely varied landscapes and weather. Unlike the savannas of Queen Elizabeth Park, I live amid spectacular mountain views. Birds of every size and description fly among the trees and nest outside the hostel. The hostel has been a huge help in growing the program. We have welcomed guests from all over the world. Once, we hosted a group of about 15 middle age short term missionary Americans -- often the most difficult guests.

"Good morning," I said after their first evening, greeting them with a smile. "I hope everything was OK?"

"It certainly was NOT!!!!!!" said a grumpy man with his hands on his hips.

"Oh my, I am sorry, what seems to be the problem?"

"Your birds are loud and rude early in the morning. They woke everyone up."

"I'm sorry about that as there is not much I can do about them," I said, trying to keep a straight face.

"You can cut down some of your trees that attract them," he said.

"Then we'd have the problem of no shade. Plus," I said, "the rude *hadadas* do not really spend time in the trees."

"Well, if you can't do anything about it," he grumbled, "You should give us a discount."

"Sir, at 25,000 USh, $7, I cannot really take much off. The money goes towards HIV positive orphans," I said. I have a wall with many pictures of cute kids in the program at the home that I call the "guilt" wall. Shame on me for using my kids like that!

The Tracey family were the first of many Irish donors who contributed to building the hostel and the rescue home. I met Bertie and Rachel Tracey early in my first fundraising trips. They invited me to visit and share my work that they heard about through the Jacksons. Their grown son Ashley caught meningitis as a baby. His speech is difficult, and he suffers with convulsions that prevent his being able to drive or do much. His physical presence makes many shy away. I believe his mind is completely OK, and I get along great with him.

At a small Bible group the Tracey's hosted, I spoke about my calling to Africa. Someone asked what was the hardest thing to deal with. I told them about seeing kids in horrific conditions in corners of huts who were being neglected and often starved because they had AIDS. I shared my dream to build a home where they could be cared for, loved, and educated.

As I was preparing for bed that evening, Bertie and

Rachael came in and said their hearts were touched. They handed me a check that I had to reach for my glasses to confirm the figure – 30,000 Euro. A group from Lucan Church in Ireland traveled to help with construction. With this large donation, the construction team, and the money from my late brother, I funded both my hostel and the Manna Rescue Home for children with AIDS. My ability to serve children is due to the generosity of others willing to share their blessings.

The facility would help those like Epafra, a boy who aged out of the home. YES gave him a course he requested for cutting men's hair. He was taken in by his sweet aunt who even though she had many kids of her own cared deeply for him. Unfortunately, AVR drugs were no longer working properly, and he went downhill quickly. I visited him several times. He always had a smile and upbeat attitude and much faith. One Saturday morning, his aunt phoned and said Epafra was asking for me and was in bad shape. He lived quite a ways out in the village and was in a small mud house on a mattress on the floor. I sat on the edge of the mattress and talked and prayed with him. His mind was clear even though his body was shutting down fast.

Right as I was getting ready to leave, he said "Adyeeri, He is here in the room!"

"Who is?" I asked.

"Jesus is with me," he said.

Epafra died in the next few minutes. I left the house quite broken up. Both courage and faith are strong here.

We finally completed and registered the Manna Rescue Home (MRH), which had kept Epafra healthy for as long as possible, in 2008. Word of the home traveled around the area. By the time we opened, 30 kids were waiting. Some were in dire need. What a blessing to be able to feed and care for them.

How we've grown! Now I wear so many hats.

I'm a manager. I oversee staff for the YES hostel and office, for the Manna Rescue Home orphanage, and the vocational school still being developed – twenty-nine people total. The orphanage is overseen by my now program coordinator, David Tumwiine, so my role is more about decision making. The office has me going long hours as we open three days a week for students with challenges who need extra help. I also have the 56-bed hostel. The hostel supports much of our work with guests staying from all over the world. That is a story in and of itself.

On occasion, I'm a counselor and even a judge.

Peter Nyakahuma, the youngest of eight kids, lost both parents through AIDS. His grown siblings were married and didn't want to bother with him. He was surviving by running errands for different households on the Kabarole cathedral grounds. In payment, the tenants gave him food. He managed to attend primary school off and on. When he got sick with malaria, he was alone and scared. I ended up taking care of him. I made sure he got more to eat as he was getting only one meal a day, and I started paying his school fees. Fast forward several years – I was in my office at the hostel with sponsors visiting from California. Peter came in, now at Senior 4, with a doctor bill, requesting money to pay it. The bill was for 3,000 Ush, but he had forged it to look like thirty thousand – poorly forged. I looked at the forged bill and quietly told him to leave and to not come back until he wanted to be honest with me. He was embarrassed with the visitors there and slunk out. One of the California ladies who was there when Peter brought the forged bill told the people back home that I was terrible and mean with a "poor orphan" kid and refused to help him with needed medicines. Anyhow, Peter returned later and dropped to his knees, begging me to forgive him, which of course I did. A few years later, I went to his ordaining into the Brothers of St. Joseph, a Catholic group of Brothers trained in different skills. At the end of the ceremony, they called for parents who wanted photos to come forward. Peter searched the crowd until he saw me and started calling, "Mom, come get a photo with me!"

Sometimes as judge, I go against my own rules and support families with more than just school fees.

For example, I met Bright Herbert when he was about 12 years old and in Primary 6. He had one sister and two brothers. His mother Akiiki Beatrice Bagambaki had a severe case of TB as well as AIDS. When I met the family, Beatrice was praying she would live long enough to know her kids were OK. I offered to pay school fees for them when she went to Kampala for TB treatments. Twelve-year-old Bright was head of the family for the next 8 months. When Beatrice came back, she was desperately ill with AIDS. Beatrice became so sick, I decided to buy her ARV medicines which the government still was not providing. They made a huge difference, and after three months she went onto a free hospital program. Bright helped me with little things around the house. Beatrice became stronger and later became an employee at the MRH and is now healthy.

By now you understand that the whole family was a part of my life. Bright was in Senior 4, the deciding school year for future education. My program is strict concerning school riots. Anyone involved will be removed without question. School riots can get completely out of control. Bright's school had a terrible riot. Cars were burned, lives threatened, and the police countered with live bullets. Bright was expelled as a leader of the strike. I called his mom in to sit as we came to a decision. Painfully, I was fully ready to put him off the program. I also included a school official on this decision. We learned Bright did not organize nor participate in the strike, but he refused to give the names of the ones who were involved. I completely understand why he would not tell on his fellow students. We decided to let him stay in the program. Consequently, he had to take the Secondary 4 exams in a different location from the school with a policeman present. His mother had to find the money. He passed well, and we continued supporting him in a different school for A Level Senior 5 and 6 which leads to university. He did so well he got a government scholarship in accounting, and he now is one of my best employees at YES.

Unfortunately, some situations do not end as well. A few former students who were expelled from the program have since come to see me, and actually thanked me for being so strict. Others have gone on to become street thugs and thieves.

I hope I never sound like I am here for the "poor ignorant natives" as so many people talk and act like. I get questions from my friends asking about shootings and climate change and other world problems. These days, I don't think anyone from the States can cast stones. I do NOT put up with nonsense from the kids. I am TOUGH when they cheat or lie. I have heard that my title is MMM for mean *mzungu* mama. I pretend to be annoyed, but truly the name makes me smile (behind closed doors, of course). We do not need thieves or liars, and it is up to them to make a difference. With my kids, I try hard to make them appreciate their country and tell them that they are the future of Uganda.

My most important hat – I am a fundraiser which mostly consists of keeping sponsors happy – far from easy. Many seem to think they are the only one for whom I need to keep track of their kid. They get upset about kids getting low grades. Most have no clue concerning the hard life led here, what these children endure – hunger, poor sanitation, children raising children, sickness. Without fundraising, the program couldn't go on. In this role, I'm also a part-time hostess. At times, interested donors stay with me in my apartment. Recently, I drove a donor the 3-hour trip to Queen Elizabeth National Park. We saw only a tiny fraction of the rich biodiversity; savannah, bushland, wetlands, and lush forests or of the 96 species of mammals, including hippos, elephants, lions, leopards and hyenas, as well as chimps. We missed the tree-climbing lions – females who enjoy the long, hot afternoons snoozing in fig trees in the remote Ishasha sector.

We did see the beautiful and varied landscape as we drove first along the foot of the Rwenzori Mountain chain and slowly dropped down until we were coming into the vast rift valley. We saw several crater lakes along with a couple of salt lakes where salt is harvested. The rift valley is what most people envision to be Africa with the huge herds of cob -- small deer-like animals; water bucks--large as a cow--water buffalo; and the large Lake Edward and Lake Albert joined by the Kazinga channel. There we took a tourist boat trip and saw elephants, hippos, crocodiles, water buffalo and birds of every description. It is amazing to be in such a different environment in less than 3 hours. The valley is much hotter than the mountains, but the people are still the same friendly and hospitable people. This particular sponsor is a businessman, and is helping set up a vocational center trust, so the long, truncated trip was well worth it.

I can't do this work alone. Bright Herbert, our accountant, is so much more than an employee. He cares for each kid and each situation. He often works overtime, running to a village with some food for a family struggling to make it or checking at the hospitals when someone is admitted. He handles large amounts of money and can be completely trusted. That in and of itself is huge when people here have extended families, most in need. He has a sense of humor, and we have some good laughs in the office. Laughing is needed when we face heavy, serious situations. He gets my sarcasm and is pretty good at it himself (perhaps I should include understanding sarcasm and weird humor for new applicants).

I get myself in trouble because I become way too attached to employees and involved with their lives. This makes it hard at times to be their boss.

We are part of the community. Beatrice Bagambaki, Bright Herbert's mom, and I met early on when I first moved to the village. She needed help with her family of four children, but she never pushed. A widow with AIDS and TB, she struggled to keep her kids fed. She couldn't afford the new antiretroviral drugs. I managed to get her started on drugs and bought them for her until they became free. In gratitude, she came to the house when she was strong enough and helped me with washing and cleaning. She was also there for me when I was sick. We sort of took care of each other back in those days. She is now doing incredibly well and is the house mother at MRH (her four kids are adults with successful lives).

We care for the children, gather sponsors, and work to get some children adopted. Sheila and Mica Smith had two girls and a boy and decided that they wanted to adopt a kid who needed a home. Sheila and I emailed back and forth, and she said she wanted a spunky girl. That describes Brenda, a little girl who came into the home half-starved and neglected, but even as a small kid, no one pushed her around. She was fun and silly, full of life but hard to make mind. She was perfect and is now a teen and doing great. The transition can be a struggle. Sheila and Micah found Brenda crying one night. At first, she wouldn't tell them why but finally confessed she worried about her brother Joseph. His aunt and grandmother were drinkers who would beat him for no reason. We were sending him to school, but we found him in bad shape several times before a teacher agreed to care for him if we could help with food costs. The Smiths came and adopted him too.

There is so much to do. So many children to help. Families waiting to find each other. I wonder how long I can keep up this pace. My heart is willing, but sometimes my body won't cooperate.

Chapter 18

Health is Wealth

I woke up one morning, during the pivotal 2008 when so much was at stake getting MRH up and running, in terrible pain and barely able to walk. Fort Portal lacked the resources to help me, so friends got me to Kampala. I received an MRI and other mobility tests. The doctors informed me I had osteoporosis and ruptured discs. They did their best for me with extensive therapy – painkillers, massage, physical therapy, and walking. There was little else they could do. Back in Fort Portal, I was fit with a body brace made with plaster which supported my back. The brace was terribly hot, yet the security felt good. I could get around without fear of a sudden pang which would land me on my derriere. Comforting as that was, under advisement, I started using it less in order to develop the muscles I needed to support my back.

My personal physical challenges do not compare to the disruption disease can cause to the community. Before the worst of my back pain started, Ebola hemorrhagic fever - the disease where people bleed to death, broke out in Bundibugyo which is just on the other side of the mountains from where I live. In farming communities where protein is scarce, people were infected with Ebola when exposed directly to wildlife such as fruit bats, gorillas, chimpanzees and duikers, a kind of deer. Dissuading the local people from wild game is difficult as other food sources are expensive. Then, when someone does die of Ebola, danger comes from the way people handle the burial. The dead body is still highly contagious. Even though Ebola is not airborne, the whole area went into a panic. The *mzungu* tourist population dropped to almost zero (yes, I stayed). At the start of the scare, only a handful of people came to the hostel for movie night. Soon, all meetings were cancelled, and the president banned the practice of shaking hands. He considered declaring a state of emergency. As if this country didn't have enough problems. We dreaded a tremendous loss of lives, not from Ebola but from fear to get treatment for anything. When there was talk of bringing some patients over from Bundibugyo, the nurses and doctors abandoned the sick patients with no care.

When I passed near the hospital, I saw patients leaving, carrying their mattresses and still very sick. Unfortunately, healthcare workers are often the first victims of outbreaks. Most of the nurses ran away and some of the doctors too. They could not risk their lives when so many were the sole support of their extended families. A wonderful Christian doctor from a Bundibugyo hospital died of Ebola. Outside the isolation wards, staff lacked rubber gloves or gowns. Fourteen health care workers from the Bundibugyo hospital were infected with the virus, and four of them died. The World Health Organization (WHO) and Ministry of Health mobilized. There was talk of quarantining western Uganda, but fortunately it never happened. This would have also kept goods such as sugar, soap, salt, toilet paper, and on and on from reaching us. Soon we would be dependent on what we could grow. A quarantine would close the petrol stations that provide cooking gas. Even with this mess, an Irish man came for ten days to teach Rose and me more about bookkeeping software. He risked being stuck here for Christmas.

We experienced similar outbreaks in 2012 and in 2018, which is ongoing. Now we have Ebola Treatment Units throughout the region. Better news, an experimental vaccine is proving successful. The current cases are located in the Congo with the exception of a few cases that had traveled to Kasese.

In December of 2009, I visited Carolyn from Germany for Christmas. Travel is always a challenge. With back problems, it is more so. Snow in Germany caused the plane from the UK to head back because the Dusseldorf airport closed. I finally managed to get out on Christmas Eve and had a wonderful Christmas Day with Carolyn and her family.

Being on the equator, Uganda has temperate, wet weather. Rarely below 65°F or above 85°F. I love the thunderstorms. I have an outside deck on my apartment and often sit out in the dark and watch the lightning show. The day storms also are spectacular. The day will be hot and sultry without a stirring of air, then the sky darkens, and a beautiful cool breeze comes through. Then, the sky suddenly goes dark as night. The breeze turns to a whipping wind and the world explodes in torrential downpours and wild lightning and thunder. There is something about the power that fills me. Of all the places I have traveled, I have never seen a thunderstorm like the ones we have here in Uganda.

We do get lots of rain, between 40 and 80 inches a year. All rain – no snow. Frolicking (as well as one can with a brace) in snow with Carolyn and her family was a delight. The cold made the brace more bearable. Getting a bit pampered didn't hurt. I'm grateful for hot showers, not having to buy and cook food daily, clothes washers and dryers. Don't get me wrong, I'd rather be in Uganda than anywhere else, though. Children's smiles more than compensate for the lack of pizza. Still, I'm not one to turn down a treat now and then.

The trip wasn't entirely (or even mostly) for leisure. I made several presentations. Because of the holidays, fewer people were interested than I'd come to expect. I did have plenty of snow to enjoy and many great visits with friends I'd met through the years. I flew to Ireland next. Again, they had more snow than normal. I visited the Jacksons, the Tracey family – Racheal, Bertie and

Ashley Tracey, Kathy and Patrick Davey and many others. I met Keith and Sinead Talbot who sponsored one of our kids, Atusasire Tomas who is now a successful medical clinical officer. Heavy snow canceled one talk, and I nearly froze at another. I started to wish I was back with the gorillas in the constantly warm weather and mist and rain.

By gorillas, I mean the wonderful animals, not the rebel guerillas. By 2008, things had lessened to an angry simmer, so no more war, officially. Even though I'd escaped physically unharmed, my body managed that all by itself, I did bear traces of the ordeal. While at a friend's house, firecrackers startled me from sleep. I fell out of the bed and rolled under it before I fully woke up. Even in another country, I cringe from any sudden or loud noise. So, I guess I did have some underlying fears.

I returned home to Uganda on January 15, 2010. I was happy and comforted to be back with my program, Ugandan friends, and the kids. I love my European and American friends and enjoy visiting the modern world but no longer feel at home outside of Uganda. There is a song that says,

> "This world is not my home; I'm just passing through.
>
> My treasures are laid up somewhere beyond the blue.
>
> The angels beckon me from Heaven's open door
>
> And I can't feel at home in this world anymore..."

That is so true. I will never fit completely in Uganda as a *mzungu* and yet no longer fit in the developed world either.

In February of 2011, the pain in my back forced me to travel abroad again. All those years of abusing my body were catching up to me by this point. I hoped to get help in California while I stayed with friends, Tara and Russel Karaviotis. Unfortunately, my Medicare wouldn't help unless I was admitted to a hospital. Russell drove me to the ER and told them I was in bad shape. The staff refused to admit me. I spent some time getting the correct medical insurance, but it was too late for that trip.

While waiting around, I found my first cousins on the internet, Maurice, Barbara and Norman. I had never met any of my extended family. After finding I truly was their long-lost cousin, they invited me to fly down and spend some time with them. I enjoyed meeting them, including the "black sheep" who is an amazing artist. Norman was full of fun and exasperated his rather proper siblings. We understood each other, though.

"So, you're the crazy relative who is bent on saving the poor blacks of Africa," he said when we met.

"Well, crazy – maybe, but as for saving the Africans, they spend more time saving me," I said. "And you must be my cousin who is out to drive the rest of his family nuts." We both laughed and got on famously.

He was outrageous and said so many things

maddening to his more reserved, wealthy relatives. He lived in an area where many African Americans were in dire poverty. He helped many pull themselves up with business loans. He had a black lady working for him, and the two seemed to take great pleasure in insulting each other. Despite his unorthodox behavior, he was full of love.

I also spent a couple of days with some other people who I had met in Uganda. I felt worried about spending a lot of time with any of these folks as they had not been expecting me. However, they all treated me great. Perhaps I was the only one worried. Anyhow, I flew home without any more medical help and just continued with the daily running of YES.

By 2013, my health caused me to slow down at what seemed the time I needed to be most alert and engaged.

The hostel saw some theft, and I fired a strong suspect. Even now, years later I hesitate to mention a name as I don't want to believe anyone would steal from those in such need. Setting aside my own sense of betrayal, I had the strong memory of accusing my door thief, saving him from stoning then worrying about his family for six months. This time, I quietly let the person go.

One of the boys who lived at the rescue home, David, died. Death is common in a place where war, refugees, poverty, corruption and AIDS are endemic. These shining little faces come to us too thin, scared, and weak. Often, they've been alone or shunted from place to place for much of their lives. We provide food, medication, clean bed and clothes, education, and love. Still, some who come to us are only visitors already on their way home.

By May 2013, I could no longer tolerate the pain. My friends the Karaviots gifted me a flight to them in California. My health insurance was now valid. I got an appointment with Dr. Jay H. Rosenburg. After some tests, he decided that I needed neck surgery! That was a bit alarming, but I went ahead with Dr. Frank J. Coufal.

While I was in the hospital getting my neck surgery, Chris Ategeka, who grew up in my program, drove all the way down from San Francisco. He put the visit on Facebook, and two different ladies who I used to teach riding to showed up as well.

I stayed with Mukoto Houck and her husband Joel for a couple of weeks because they were closer to the rehab center. Sarah Char met up with me and took me out to do tourist stuff which was great. I attended the Station Church and was impressed with the young couple running it.

I finally came home mid-July even though I was not feeling well yet. I arrived with a bad tooth and headed directly to Dr. Deo Mawano, my dentist, and had a root canal. Finally, I hired a private car for home as I was not up for public transportation.

I tried another fundraising trip abroad for a vocational center in 2014. I had come back from my 2013 neck surgery and finalized purchase on some land. I had the vocational school construction plans drawn and went on an extended fundraising trip to Ireland,

Germany, California, and Colorado so I could proceed. I ended up going over the Rocky Mountains from Grand Junction to Denver five times in one trip. Once by train – beautiful but long as the train got stuck in the mountains; once by air – bumpy but pretty flight; and three times by car. Unfortunately, I did not raise enough on this trip to finish developing my vocational school.

In 2016, my health was worse, so I again flew to the US to seek medical help. I first stopped in Skaneateles, NY, where I had run my first stable and lived for many years. The trip provided closure for me, seeing old friends and the place where I had so many experiences.

I then headed to Florida for laser surgery for my back only to learn that Medicare would not cover laser treatment. Even to get approved for care, I was told that I needed to live in the States for at least six months. I could not leave my work for so long, so I ended up staying with Sheila and Micah Smith, who had adopted Brenda and Joseph from my program. What a pure joy seeing my kids who have been adopted by families in the US on Facebook and even in person. Several came together and met with me in Florida. To see them now leading healthy and happy lives fills my heart. All the death, murders, wars, sickness, thefts, and corruption cannot override the immense joy of working here in Uganda.

Sheila decided I needed a proper vacation. I always wished to go on a roller coaster, but Sheila worried about my back. Instead, she and Micah took me to a water park, I rode my first water slide – it was great! They also took me to a friend's house who had a horse, and I was able to take my last ride. Sheila is great with her five kids. We have so much fun together even though she is young enough to be my daughter. Micah is a serious man who runs an insurance business and a kind loving father who is so patient with the kids. Both Brenda and Joseph were older when they were adopted. Together they have faced many issues and are doing such a good job. They are dear friends who I feel blessed to have in my life.

By mid-2017, I could hardly walk. I had yet another MRI and was told things were critical. I flew to India for treatment. I went to a hospital in New Delhi where, after extensive investigation, they did surgery. The surgeons inserted six screws and a spacer into my spine. Even with kind doctors, the experience was scary. I could not speak the language of most the people I encountered, and many could not speak English. For about six weeks, I felt alone amongst millions.

By January of 2018, my pain was debilitating. I sent an x-ray to the doctor in India. He phoned me immediately saying, "Come to New Delhi right away. Things look bad!" I couldn't face being alone again.

After several emails, my dear friends Ben and Jess Weiderholt in Colorado insisted I come there, and they would set me up with a good surgeon. Jess is a founder of the Crazy Love fair trade program run through YES. Jess is a strong woman who home schools all seven of their kids. Ben is the quiet one who has the patience of Job and is a bit of a baseball fanatic with their five boys. He works within Denver's health department. My condition was now listed as an emergency so Medicare would cover it.

My friends in the area drove me around and were a great help as I prepared for my second major surgery in a six-month period. The surgery was tough, and recovery was also hard. Despite her mad schedule, Jess came to the hospital daily. Both Ben and Jess were there for me during some terribly painful and scary times. My spinal cord sprung a leak right after surgery, and my condition was critical for some time. The Weiderholts were so, so good to me for the two months I was with them. I will be forever grateful.

At long last, I was ready, desperate, to go home. I miss many people in the US but no longer feel like I belong there. Just going to Costco or Walmart feels overwhelming. Why on earth do people need so much stuff? I will never understand.

One of my barn kids from Maui came back into my life. Nichole Tongg lives with her partner Sue Bauineau in New Jersey where they run a pet supply shop. A love for animals is lifelong! Nichole had already helped me with a GoFundMe for my medical costs. When I wanted to come home, I found last minute tickets expensive, and I asked for suggestions on Facebook. Nichole phoned me while I was in rehab and said she wanted to give me her extra miles. I didn't know what she meant until she booked me home on a first-class flight! I find it amazing how my past and present lives seem to keep coming together. Finally, on March 19,

2018, I headed home to Uganda. I have no desire to head anywhere again for a long time, if ever.

Chapter 19

Acceptance

W hy would I ever leave? There is too much to do.
Chris Ategeka is the unwitting instigator of a
current project. A donor connected with me through
the sister of one of our adopting parents. The sister
was canvassing door to door for a political cause. She
and her companion fellow canvasser, Jim West, got
into a conversation about Africa. She told him that
her sister Martha had taken in a student from Uganda,
Christopher. Jim wanted to know more. He and I
began corresponding. At that time, I was searching for
a way to develop non-academic training for the many
young people who struggle with traditional education.
Study here is difficult for anyone who has a hard time
with language acquisition. Primary 4 onward is taught
in English.

Jim traveled to Uganda, and together we searched

for land and bought the present place just outside of Fort Portal. We had our vocational school plans drawn up, and that's when I took the trip in 2014 to raise funding for this project. After a slow and convoluted process to get started, the Amaani Rwenzori vocational training program is in place. The program sends students to different places for training, and its beautiful campus provides for four social businesses. The campus hosts a hairdressing and beauty salon, sewing and design training, a ceramics studio with kilns and wheels, and a coffee shop.

Amaani Rwenzori means "power for Rwenzori." Here in the Kabarole district, we are in the Rwenzori mountains. Beauty is mixed with poverty everywhere. Yet even though the majority of people live in abject poverty, they know how to enjoy life. Even if they come from a mud hut, they have clean clothes and shoes and take pride in looking good. In town, they tend to dress better than most visiting *bzungu*. Their clothes might be threadbare and ragged, but they try hard. If, however, you drive in the countryside, you see many people are in rags, especially the kids. So many visitors are horrified when they see dirty kids in rags and barefoot. People who criticize need to remember that families do not have running water, and soap is expensive. The adults, too, appear ragged from working in the fields and doing dirty work. See these families at church or a function, and the kids are clean and dressed in their "good" clothes.

I must say, with all respect and thankfulness, that

the visiting NGOs can themselves be a problem. I know that sounds terribly cynical, but I have seen too much of the "White Savior," colonization attitude. Many educated Ugandans agree, but others clamor for the huge salaries international NGOs can afford. Local NGOs such as mine cannot begin to compete. Once an employee gets a chance at the big time, they leave. These international organizations never listen to the local experts. They usually come in for a few years then leave behind a huge white elephant that cannot sustain itself. In one instance, I voiced a criticism, and the expat manager replied, "what they get is better than nothing, and they are only Africans."

One wonders why anyone with such a condescending attitude would even work in a developing country. Often expats take salaries that would be huge even in their own country. I heard of a manager receiving 12,000 euro a month! They get free, luxurious housing, drive big vehicles, yet what trickles down to the community often is not even 40%. I had a year contract with an NGO to provide school lunches. At the end of the year, a Ugandan manager came to me.

"Madame, we have worked well, have we not?" he said.

"Yes, thank you, we have fed many children this year," I said.

"Might I have some tea?" he asked, in an office, no kettle in sight.

"There is no expenditure line for tea," I said, getting to the point.

"You have been here a long time," he said. "Have you not learned to cook the books?"

While NGOs may be a challenge, so many people have come and helped from a true sense of compassion and love. Paul and Ellen Sullivan are one such couple. They found our hostel while traveling the continent in a huge camper truck equipped with solar panels and all their needs. Paul is a retired engineer from Ireland, and Ellen is a retired American school teacher. They had lived many years in Tanzania. They stayed at the hostel making mechanical repairs on the camper. We hit it off. Before they continued their journey, they came up to my apartment and asked if I could use their help as volunteers for a year. I sure could! Ellen is strongly religious and soft spoken. She is fantastic with kids and was a well-loved teacher at the MRH. She is a small and sweet lady, seemingly opposite of her husband. Paul is a bit loud and quite funny and tough acting but not tough at all. Paul designed the beautiful buildings for the campus.

Paul also wrote policies for the rescue home to ensure government compliance. The government closed hundreds of orphanages in the country because of corruption and misuse of kids. Paul is a strong and outspoken man who nevertheless took the time to listen to others. He was immediately liked by the people we serve. He did not act superior as so many missionaries do. Paul's work helped us become approved and registered as one of only 17 homes out of 400 investigated. They have since gone their way, but we are in touch by email and

Skype. I am forever grateful for our friendship.

The Ugandan people have taught me much more than I could ever teach them. Yes, our programs bring hope with education and care, but the people have taught me what is important in life. Sometimes misguided efforts get in the way. We can find it hard to understand that Ugandans live for the day and for each other. Sometimes this attitude can slow down progress because concern about the future, saving, and planning are not a priority. Ugandan ladies my age say this has not always been the case. Years of horrible dictatorship and the AIDS epidemic have taught them to just exist day to day.

A regular joy are visits from friends and sponsors. They keep me active. To keep up with them and my kids, I used to take walks around the neighborhood. Our skies are often cloudless blue. You can walk in and out of the shade of banana plants, standing taller than the brightly colored buildings. You see lush hillsides, dense with trees. You hear the call of birds and the incessant buzz of insects. When my back became too painful for me to safely walk about, Chris, on one of his surprise visits, brought me a treadmill.

My local doctor has fits. He says I should only stay quiet and still, but if I don't push myself, I think I would go downhill faster. Also, have I told you I'm stubborn?

Staying quiet isn't always an option, and I must maintain my wits. One evening, a thief broke away from three *boda* men and ran into my yard here at the hostel. The night guard shut him in the guardhouse. The *boda* men called for the thief, but I refused. Before I knew it, over 50 men were screaming at the gate, banging it with large stones, and demanding the thief. I phoned David, my field officer at the time, who drove to the police begging them to come help. They refused. "That mob might hurt us," they said. "Just let them kill the man."

I couldn't do that. By then my guard and hostel manager were so scared that they ran and hid way at the bottom of the property. I tried to calm the mob but instead had to dodge the rocks being thrown. The poor thief was terrified and actually soiled himself. I phoned a *mzungu* family and asked them to go to the police. Embarrassed, the police finally came and took the man. The *boda* men became riled, firing gunshots in the distance. I have police stories that never finish, and the vigilante mind set is always scary. You can't pick up the phone for police, fire, or ambulance here. People in developed countries don't realize how fortunate they are.

I know that I have talked of mob justice and thieves and corruption, but they are the loud minority. Again and again, I have been helped by total strangers. I am treated with much respect because here age is an honor, even to teenagers. And every once in a while, the vocal crowds (not mobs when they are helping me!) are the help one needs.

I had a field officer named Grace (yes, a man named Grace) with whom I was far from satisfied. He was stealing money, and I learned he brought kids into the program after getting paid by caregivers. After several verbal and written warnings to him, I brought proof of his stealing to the NGO board and fired him in a legal manner. A year and a half later, I received a letter from the head of the local labor board saying that I owed Grace 2,500,000 USh -- about $1000 back then -- for firing him unlawfully. I provided the warnings and the final dismissal letter that I had given to Grace. After several exchanges, I received an official looking letter demanding the 2.5 million. I ignored the letter. Several days later, when Rose, David, my present field officer, and I were talking with an elderly lady about the six orphans she was struggling to care for, two armed police and a man in a suit entered the office.

"You are under arrest," said the man in the suit.

"Show me the warrant," I demanded. They waved something at me but wouldn't give me time to get my glasses on to read it.

One officer rudely grabbed my arm, pulled me to the police car and shoved me in. David and Rose immediately ran for the program motorcycle while Florence, another employee, hurried to her car. These folks followed right behind the police car as people have been known to disappear in such situations. Instead of taking me to the police station, the trio took me to the rather grungy office of the labor officer. Papers were in piles everywhere. A chicken scratched in a corner. Jagged glass stuck out from broken windows. I told Rose to call someone for help as she waited outside on the rickety porch.

"Sit down," the labor officer yelled at me. "You are in a court of law."

"Right?!" I said as I handed my phone to Rose through the broken window. Then I sat on a tottering chair in front of his ridiculously fancy desk for such a decrepit office. The labor officer sat with his arms folded above his fat belly.

"Now madam, when are you going to pay me your money?"

"Never--sir," I replied with definite sarcasm.

"You will go to prison!"

I put my wrists together as if in handcuffs and said, "We go."

He stared at me, then stood up so fast that he sent his fancy chair flying backwards. He told the police, one was a lady, to watch me until he got back. He stormed out of the office and flew off on his motorcycle. The two police looked at each other. The man in the suit had disappeared.

By this time, the grandmother who had been at my office when the police arrived had run to the market to notify people of my situation, and many people were gathering on the lawn around the labor office. I was sitting on the porch with Florence, Rose, and David talking about what to do next.

"All you need to do is pay the labor officer," said one of the police. Over an hour went by.

Looking at the crowd, I saw a lady, Stella, who had been sick in the hospital pushing her way through. I was thrilled to see her as I had not expected her to survive. I stood up and started hurrying to her to hug her saying "Stella!" with a big smile when I heard a sort of click, scrunch sound behind me. Stella gasped with large eyes. I turned around, and the lady cop had cocked and aimed her MK47 at my head. I froze.

"Put that thing down!" I managed in a strong voice, and she did. I was really shaking and started scolding her. "I am old enough to be your mom or even your grand mom. Is this how you treat your elders?"

She looked ashamed and said, "I am sorry, Mama."

By then the crowd had grown to about 50 people, all talking about what was going on. The policeman said he was tired of waiting for the man in the suit, and that they just needed to take me to lock up. Florence was by then having fits and saying that David needed to get the money and pay.

"NO WAY!!!" I said. The police started walking me to the courthouse about a quarter of a mile away. The whole crowd of people followed which made the police nervous. On reaching the courthouse, I was pushed into a holding cell.

"You are highly welcome madam," said one of the three dirty, smelly, barefoot men in the room.

I was locked in the cell for about two hours while the crowd continued growing outside. More police arrived, worried about a riot. Professor Rugumayo, a retired distinguished politician, came over to the officer who arrested me and demanded to see the warrant. Instead of giving it to him, they unlocked the door, told me to come out, and then took off at a run. The crowd cheered and made a huge noise while I stood there rather overwhelmed.

"Where did the police go?" I asked Professor Rugumayo.

"Do you want them to come back?" he laughed.

I was free to go but the incident was far from over. The man in the suit (from the labor office) was absolutely furious. The word was out that he would get me again into a cell where he would "get me hurt." Florence continued to beg me to pay up, but I am way too stubborn to pay an unfair money. I was quite fearful for some weeks and worked out escape routes from my apartment in case the police showed up again. Things got complicated, and the situation reached the President of Uganda, Yoweri Museveni, who warned the people involved to leave me alone. The two police officers, court bailiff, and the man in the suit confessed to being off duty when the incident occurred and that they were offered 100,000 Ush each if they could get me to pay up. I could have sued the government and police over the whole ordeal, but that wouldn't have been a good idea if I wanted to continue with the work my program was doing for the kids. The lady cop, who pointed her gun at my face, would see me here and there and always greet me with "How are you, Mama?" and a big smile. I see the man in the suit from time to time. He acted as if nothing had ever happened. He even came to the hostel a few times asking to use my ping pong table.

The story was much talked about around town, especially the lady cop pulling her gun on me and my telling her off. That was just pure adrenaline, not courage. This story is sort of funny now but wasn't at all funny at the time. I shared this story with a visiting mission group, and they criticized me for my weak faith because I said I was scared by the experience. Sigh. I wonder how they would like an MK47 pointed at their heads?

We must have a sense of humor here in Uganda, or we couldn't last. Life here is a series of joys and mishaps – the kinds of things which make you smile and thank God for the beauty of the hills and the beauty of the souls around you. Writing this book makes me pause to appreciate all I have in my life even as I revisit the challenges.

I am saddened when we lose a child to AIDS, even more so when we lose friends. A week after we lost David, the boy from MRH, Adolf Rwampere died. Adolf was a wonderful neighbor in the Kasusu village. He was deformed with a huge humpback and a bone poking out of his chest. The poor man was shunned by many because of his deformities. Many villagers considered him bewitched. His parents kept him hidden while his brother went to school. He barely knew any English, but we hit it off anyhow. He loved looking through my National Geographic magazines and would point out pictures of cities even though he never roamed further from home than Fort Portal. One day, he couldn't wake me up as I was down with malaria and a high fever. He walked 4 miles to a hospital and returned with a nurse. Another time, he planted flowers on the side of the path to my front door and was so proud when I came home and saw them. I simply enjoyed his presence. He had an innocent sweetness about him. He became a close friend and an employee at MRH. He had five kids who adored him. The little ones followed him everywhere. He died when they were 6, 8,9, 11 and 14 years old, and I have tried to help them since. Three of them are now in school. There are so many families of kids with no adults. They are amazing in how they can manage to get by with so little.

On March 15, 2013, my best friend in the states, Jeanne Grozsbach died. I met Jeanne by mail back when I was first in Uganda. I had come across an old magazine called *American Farm Wife* with tasty sounding recipes. Most needed ingredients I could not get such as canned soups or cream cheese. I wrote her a letter asking for any suggestions for cooking with only basic foods. I was overwhelmed with wonderful suggestions. From Iowa, Jeanne mailed me a book titled *Back to Basics* that to this day I find useful. I sent a letter of thanks, and so our friendship began. Because I was quite lonely and a bit scared, her letters meant a lot. On a trip back to the States, I met Jeanne and Joe on their farm. Jeanne was completely a "farmer's wife" with her house decorated in old farm Americana. A normal conversation with her church group and local friends revolved around cows and corn.

Jeanne was fascinated by a different life and world. About the same age as me, she bounced around with energy. When I started connecting by email with an international NGO--World Wildlife Federation, I convinced Jeanne and Joe to get a computer. The dumb then started teaching the dumb. I tried to show them basic things as I was learning on my first computer, too. We went from emailing once a week to daily if power was on in town. Jeanne was my friend who let my brother Henry know how ill I was while managing my other brother Bill's estate. Jeanne was interested in everything I was doing and was not judgmental. I shared doubts and fears with her.

She also was fascinated by Moses who was studying medicine in Ukraine. Jeanne arranged for him to do a 6-month practical study with a doctor friend in a hospital there in Iowa. They became close friends. I am continually amazed at how different people from different chapters of my life have connected with each other from all over the world. She had an infectious laugh and was so very alive. Unfortunately, she also smoked nonstop.

Her death came the same month I fought double pneumonia. I thought I was handling the news OK. The next morning on March 16, my memory is vague here, I remember feeling sick and driving to the medical clinic. From this point, I relate only what I was later told. I walked into the clinic and demanded an x-ray. The people at the clinic were all familiar to me. I always have greeted them by name, but they said I acted like a stranger. They tried to say that my x-ray already showed my pneumonia, but I was insistent. They complied, even though the doctor was not there. They told me the x-ray had not changed. I walked out without saying anything – again, unlike me. I have no memory of driving home, and that alone is scary if you ever saw what driving here is like. Remember my first days in Uganda?

I was apparently sick to my stomach because I was found sitting in my chair with a mixing bowl on my lap, vomiting, screaming, and crying. Florence Kisembo, my hostel manager and close friend, came running in asking me what was wrong. I looked at her and demanded, "Who are you!!!???" Then asked, "Where am I?" I have no memory whatsoever of any of this. Florence found someone to drive me to the clinic I had just left. She does not drive. The man and Florence forced me to walk to the car. I kept asking them who they were and where were they taking me. I reached the clinic for the second time that day. Dr. Henry, a close friend, was there this time. He said I acted completely crazy, demanding to know what was going on. One funny thing, I had to go to the bathroom badly. The toilet I was taken to was not flushed. I took the top off the tank and reached to pull the wire to flush it. I proceeded to fix it before closing it. I am often fixing toilets here at the hostel, too. That action sure had everyone laughing even in their concern. They then took me to a bed, and because I was strongly resisting, they gave me a shot that knocked me out and put an IV drip on me as I looked dehydrated.

The same day at about 7 pm, I woke up completely normal. I found many people standing around my bed, Mariam Kluge, Father Paschal Kabura, Florence, and several other friends. I was quite confused but knew everyone and knew where I was. The clinic staff were all happy I started greeting them by name. Dr. Henry was stumped. Dr. Moses was already driving to Fort Portal to take me to his hospital in Kampala where there were more tests available. This episode scared me so much because I was afraid that I would have to repeat the trip to California where I ended up getting neck surgery for a vertebra pinching my spinal cord. I didn't have it in me to do it again. They ventured that my episode in Fort Portal sounded like Transient Global Amnesia brought on by a combination of tension and lack of blood flow.

David died. Adolph died. The hostel was robbed
And the Moriel Ministries came to town.

Moriel Ministries is a fervently devout Christian organization with charities around the world. I find myself grateful for all the work they do while finding their prejudices against "theologically deviant expressions of Christendom" distasteful. Jacob Prasch and David Royle were investigating my NGO to be one of their beneficiaries, but they did not approve of my friendship with Muslims and Catholics. Years later, Jacob would write me saying that having a pro-abortion person on my board and associating with Muslims was "the reason God had not provided me the funds to retire." First, who are they to judge? Second, asking God to help me retire is not part of my wish list. Finally, doesn't God want us to give and accept love as we work to care for his children on earth? I defended my Muslim friend, a hardworking gift to YES, and as politely as I could thanked them for the donation.

I love how there is no obvious problem between Christians and Muslims here. Eid Mubarak is a day of celebration for Muslim communities. This year, two pretty little girls who live across the road from me came to my door all dressed in frilly clothes with a plate filled with traditional foods from their culture. Their family escaped horrible conflicts from Yemen and now live in peace here. My neighbors always bring me a treat on their big holidays. Likewise, I make sure they get Christmas cookies and cakes from me. Their sect requires the ladies to completely cover their faces when outside of the home, but as neighbors we always wave and smile at each other. As I was coming back from church one Sunday afternoon, huge crowds of Muslim people and crowds of Christians were waving and laughing and wishing each other well. The Catholic Church is next door to the mosque. As parishioners walked from the church, they were mixing with the Muslim celebrations exchanging smiles and handshakes.

Not only on holidays, but there are also always people, people, people everywhere. Wherever I walk takes a bit of time as I am often stopping and talking with someone. People here are never in a hurry and are patient when stuck in long queues. Chatting with any stranger, even clowning around, is completely acceptable. Once a young woman who was staying with me and I visited a health clinic. A fully armed soldier stood guard outside the door.

"Madame, can I marry your daughter?" he asked.

Without missing a beat, I replied, "I do not think you can afford her bride price."

"How much would that be, Madame?"

"At least 25 cows and five good goats," I replied.

"I could possibly square that up," he answered.

My visitor was horrified. She said in a loud whisper, "What are you trying to do to me?"

At that, the soldier and I broke out in laughter. Later she asked if I knew the man. I said that I didn't. She said my "over friendliness" seemed dangerous. I guess that sort of joking around wouldn't happen in a developed country, but I love how we can do such here.

You also find masses of jubilant people at church. I attend the Sunday service at the Church of Uganda Cathedral, right outside of Fort Portal. I pick up my friend Ateenyi and her 4 grandchildren who live about a mile from me, leaving the house about 8:40 am for the 9 am service. Finding a seat is hard if we are at all late. When full, between 900 to 1000 people attend the service, and most of the time I am the only *mzungu*. Today, September 1, 2019, the church was packed, but we managed to squeeze in halfway to the back. After the clergy and choir come in and we sing the first hymn, and the young people sing lively songs. Today, the church was hopping with so much joy. As I sang along, I watched people clapping, dancing, and almost jumping with the dynamic songs of praise. I smiled because I have heard that the Anglican Church is stodgy and dull. Not in Uganda!!! My body doesn't jump anymore, but I appreciate the freedom during worship to either jump around or not without judgements from anyone. That huge crowd, all praising and singing, is emotional and uplifting. After the praise singing, we hear a Bible reading that introduces the upcoming sermon. Then the children, usually 150 to 200 kids, are called forward for a blessing before they head to Sunday school.

The Cathedral is the center of what is called the diocese. As such, we often have different preachers. Many of the clergy on Karabole Hill, the diocese grounds, are friends who have been with me in difficult times. Our bishop actually worked for me many years ago as a field officer when he was just a priest. Today, a retired archbishop gave a deep and moving sermon. I saw a couple of people in tears.

After the sermon there are announcements and – grumble, grumble – sometimes fundraising. YES and the church rely heavily on donations **of all kinds**. A couple from Texas who joined a short-term mission decided to gift our Manna Rescue Home (MRH) with a milk cow. When I saw the cow, I was a bit shocked to see that she had never calved, and she had no milk at all. I asked a local farmer if she could be bred with his bull. He agreed but said she would never give much milk as she was more of a beef cow. At the couple's good-bye party, they asked if the kids were enjoying the milk. I told them everything. They were furious with the seller. They demanded a good milk cow or their money back. We eventually did get a milk cow. When I recall this generosity, I sort of chuckle because I would have thought anyone could see the cow had no udder – especially a Texan.

Today, the church is raising money to build real bathrooms with flushing toilets. Now there is only a deep pit latrine. I never drink much coffee on Sunday mornings. Service ends with the last hymn as the choir and clergy leave, and then we all pile out. If we ever have an earthquake and people leave in a panic, I fear the outcome. Even with three doorways, the entries are crowded. The church has four services on Sunday. When missionaries come here to bring the gospel, I sort of feel that perhaps the exchange should be the other way around with Ugandans going to the US to preach. Once outside of the church, you can never hop in the car and drive off unless it is raining. There are always friends to greet.

Attending church gives me time to let go of things from the past week and energizes me for whatever I will face in the coming week. At the cathedral I am just me and not a *mzungu*. I cannot really explain why I love Uganda and call it home. But today, while in the service, I realized that I so love the church here and the people.

Chapter 20

Life and Death

In April of 2013, I was invited to the 21st birthday celebration of the Tooro *Omukama* – the king – who I had met when he was a four-year old child under the regency of John Katuramu. I had seen him off and on, watching him grow. The first time I met his mom, the queen mother, was on an Easter Sunday when an Anglican priest who was somehow related to her brought me to meet the queen at the palace. She invited me in to have a Coke and chat. The king, about 6 at that time, came in demanding candy and was quite mouthy with his mom when told it was too close to his mealtime.

"It is sometimes difficult raising a young boy who knows he is a king," the queen said when he went back outside to play.

"A kid is a kid," I laughed, "acting like any kid."

Another time, I was at a church service with the king and his mom in attendance. At some point, his mother noticed he was gone. His mortified guards found him outside playing in the dirt with a toy car. The incident made the New Vision News (local media) with photos.

I hate big crowds but felt that I should at least show my face for the king's 21st birthday. I couldn't imagine what sort of a gift I should give him, but then remembered I had a kukui nut lei from Hawaii. They used to be worn by royalty on the islands, so I dusted it off and brought it along in case gift giving would be expected. I also brought along a shell necklace, just in case.

On April 16, 2013, I made my way to the palace grounds, sitting atop the highest hill in Fort Portal. I sat among hundreds of people, more than a thousand, waiting to see *Rukirabasaija* (greatest of men) Oyo Nyimba Kabamba Iguru Rukidi IV, traditional leader of the Kingdom of Tooro, one of the seven kingdoms of Uganda. The men were dressed in fresh, white *kanzu*, a kind of tunic. The Batooro women wore a complicated style of dress called the Suuka. Three pieces, often in bright contrasting colors and patterns, include a long length of fabric wrapped around the shoulders, a knee-length dress, and an akitambi - rich fabric wrapped around the waist falling to the feet.

I was watching all the dancing and festivities when a man appeared and led me into the palace and up a circular staircase. He told me to have a seat on the sofa. A huge flat TV on the wall was showing news of the Boston Terrorist attack on the marathon. After a short while, a well-dressed lady entered – Best Kemigisa, the queen mother. She hugged me like an old friend. We sat and had a good time gossiping and laughing. Next thing the king himself walks in. I was startled but stood up and told him happy birthday. They invited me to have lunch with them. I asked the king about leaving his own celebration, and he said that at times it was nice to be just a person. He said he would get back to them but that he and his mom thought they would have me for lunch and just enjoy some quiet time. Servants then carried out many dishes of meats and vegetables and we sat around yacking like old friends. I gave him his lei and her the shells. You would have thought I gave them gold. The king is a down to earth young man and great company. He wished to some day visit Hawaii, so the lei was a great gift. To this day I still haven't figured out why I was singled out to have lunch with royalty on such an important birthday.

The land I bought in the village where I first built my house and then later converted into the Manna Rescue Home is owned by the kingdom. Back then, I didn't know enough about land titles. I was told the land belonged to John Katuramu's mother and she had decided to sell it. When I learned that it was kingdom land, I went to kingdom officials and managed to get a long-term lease on it. Both the king and his mom have visited the kids at the rescue home. I am not at all concerned that we will ever be pushed off the land. It means the world to me to have their support.

Other royal lands are less secure. The queen laid

claim on a parcel of land to develop and found squatters had moved in. When she tried to have them removed, the people rioted, trying to keep their houses. Orphans from our program came to the office telling us they were being kicked out with nowhere to go. They were a child-headed family with the 15-year-old twin boy and girl from YES and two older brothers. I took the twins with me to the palace, and Queen Best Kemigisa welcomed us into her office.

"Queen Best, we understand the land is yours, but these children were born there," I explained. "They have no extended family to go to."

"You don't know the whole story, Mama Carol," she said, turning to the twins.

"You have troubled Mama Carol," she scolded.

"Madame, my agents had offered them a place to go. These foolish kids joined the riots."

"They're only children," I said, "caught up in the anger."

"I wish it weren't so, but I'm not unsympathetic." She graciously gave us 30 million USh to help the kids find another house and land.

The Manna Rescue Home continues helping many students and kids who come in weak and sick. With love, medical and nutritional care many improve greatly. Heartbreak comes, though when kids do not make it, like Epafra. The courage and faith these kids show is inspiring.

There is much death here. It seems that there is a burial almost weekly for one of my staff to attend.

One burial that stands out in my mind is the burial of a sweet grandmother who cared for eight orphans. We were assisting her, and we had visitors from the US who I took to see her and the kids. The same evening her drug-using, drinker son came and demanded the money he insisted we left there with her. We had not left anything for her. Her son, in a drunken rage, beat her to death in front of all the kids.

The burial was three days later. I went with Rose my office worker and sweet friend as well as with a visiting Canadian who was working on a book about the courage of orphaned children. A burial in the local sense is beyond anything anyone in the developed world can imagine. The coffin was outside her small mud hut balanced between two chairs. Old tarps were tied from trees with banana fibers to cover the rickety benches that had been brought out for VIP visitors. Neighbors gathered around with many already drunk. They waited to see if her killer son would come for the burial. They planned to kill him if he did. Little speeches were given by a few people in the native language. I spoke as well. Standing near the coffin was terrible with big bottleneck flies buzzing around as the coffin dripped bodily fluids and the stench was extreme. I still associate pine smell and death smell together because they lay pine needles on the ground trying to hide the smell – it doesn't! Our visitor asked Rose why they waited so long to bury the body, and she replied casually that it prevents some cannibalistic villagers from digging her back up for a meal. The poor visitor and I turned a bit green at that thought. With prayers finished and songs sung, they finally brought the coffin to the grave dug in the banana patch for burial.

At that point, Rose came to me quite alarmed and told me the villagers were talking about killing a 2-year-old boy, son of the son who killed the grandmother, because the villagers believed he must have the same evil in his blood as his father. They were waiting until we left to throw his body into the same grave. As I am often the lone mzungu in such a situation, I find it hard to recall the orderly funerals in the States.

I had Rose call the heads of the village over and ordered them to fill in the grave while we were still there. We insisted they bring the baby to our office the next day along with the mother who was quite mad. I said that if they were not there by 9 am we would send the police to the village. They had better have the boy or they would be arrested. As soon as we returned from the burial, I went to the probation officer and told her the story and said the boy had to be brought to the babies' home in town. Sometime later I heard of a family from the US who were looking to adopt a young boy. Nyakahuma, the boy we rescued, also had a medical condition but the family were still interested. Adoptions here take a lot of paperwork, and my field officer David is good at running around getting the needed papers. Meanwhile, Nyakahuma's father was arrested for stealing a *boda* – police never searched for him for killing his mother – and he was required to sign a paper to allow his boy to be adopted. He refused to sign the papers with the hopes of being offered some money and perhaps be able to bribe his way out of prison. We didn't know how to proceed, but other prisoners who overheard the situation and learned that the man had murdered his mother took over. They killed him. This left the mother who went from normal to quite crazy frequently. In her sane mode she understood that Nyakahuma would have a better life if he were to be adopted, and she signed the required papers.

We had many kids adopted by families in the US before Uganda changed the laws making it almost impossible now to adopt. I have continued to follow the progress of these kids and have watched them become mature and happy young people. I cannot imagine how hard it must be for these kids going into such a completely different life and culture after they leave Uganda.

Things are so different here than in the Western world that even when a sponsor sees it firsthand, they might not fully grasp it. An American who visited for a week insisted that my orphans' families should have flush toilets and hot running water. I said they need food, medicine, and education first. Most villages do not have running water, so flush toilets are completely impractical and far from a priority. He was so blind, even when seeing things in person. That causes understandable anger that Ugandans keep quiet about because they need the money or support. I also had completely Western eyes when I first arrived in Uganda. I tried to keep quiet at first and learn what was needed the most. My Ugandan friends were so very helpful and patient with me. I no longer get upset because kids do not have birthday celebrations or toys from Santa for Christmas. The culture is so different, but different does not mean bad, and it needs to be honored.

Through all the transitions and ups and downs, the program keeps running. We have between 200 and 300 kids in YES from year to year. Many students have completed secondary school and continued to higher education and careers. They are doctors, engineers, teachers, lawyers, accountants, nurses and many, many other professions. Moses Magezi, who lived with me, is the head surgeon of a large hospital in Kampala and is married with three children. Christopher Ategeka was raised by a deaf, mute grandmother deep in a village. He is now a UC-Berkeley graduate, a technology expert in the US, and philanthropist in Uganda. Families in the program have hope because they see a future as their grown children improve their living standards.

We hope the same for our own families.

In May 2013, I was thrilled to have my brother and sister-in-law visit, Henry and Marlene. I enjoyed getting to know my sister-in-law and grew fond of her. Henry is a total tourist wherever he goes. His camera is almost fastened to his face. I took them to visit the Manna Rescue Home and other projects and some families. He seemed quite uncomfortable. I think he found my work hard to understand or internalize as my situation and lifestyle are far from his interests and life which consists of travel, cruises, and food at exclusive restaurants. I set up a trip to Queen Elizabeth Park and drove him around to some other beautiful areas to indulge his photography. Marlene and I talked late into the night. The strange thing with Henry is that he has almost no memory of our childhood. We had nothing in common to talk about. He did say something, though that still makes me laugh.

"I wish I had your faith," he said as he was leaving, "but I'm too intelligent."

"Thanks???" Sort of a backhanded compliment as I see it.

That's OK because my family abounds in Uganda. I do pray that someday Henry will find a closer relationship with our Lord. He is a loving person and he and Marlene have a special place in my heart.

The year my brother Henry visited, YES graduates threw a huge celebration for me for my 17th year here. Under a sunny sky with a slight breeze, they led a parade through town to the hostel where I live now. Here they gave speeches and gifts to me. One of the most precious gifts is a YouTube video with many of my students, dating back to 1998, expressing gratitude for the education and opportunities YES provided to them. They are now a teacher, doctor, veterinarian, carpenter, radio presenter, news anchor, and farming consultant each taking the time to say how our programs helped them to now help others. I was overwhelmed with so, so much love. Caregivers spoke on behalf of the younger kids, and the older children spoke for themselves. Walking through town, grown men and women stepped up to give me a hug and call me mom or gran or aunty. I am reminded of a Bible verse – Isaiah 54:

> *"Sing, barren woman, you who never bore a child;*
> *burst into song, shout for joy, you who were never in labor;*
> *because more are the children of the desolate woman*
> *than of her who has a husband," says the Lord.*
>
> *"Enlarge the place of your tent, stretch*
> *your tent curtains wide, do not hold back;*
> *lengthen your cords, strengthen your stakes.*
>
> *For you will spread out to the right and to the left;*
> *your descendants will dispossess nations and settle in*
> *their desolate cities."*

Yesterday, David, my country director picked up 49 school reports from one of our local schools. Kids were streaming in to retrieve them. Each report must be reviewed, and if the students have any issues, academically or otherwise, David counsels them. I take care of the many students who are waiting for their turn to review their reports. I give them pens, exercise books, or any school supplies they may need. During that process, a German man who I have had major issues with in the past comes into the office behaving overly sweetly because he wants to "borrow" my employee who works on the hostel compound and does minor plumbing and carpentry. I have trained him specifically for that because I am tired of running down to the hostel fixing toilets and doors and such. I agreed to his request for 1 day a week only as the young man does need the extra money.

Back to the craziness. Students continued to stream

in, several begging to be allowed into a boarding school. We do not have enough money for all their requests. Another student came in with failing grades. When I questioned her, she broke into tears. I took her into another room to settle her down and have a talk when a mom came in crying hysterically because her daughter with AIDS is in bad shape in the hospital. This poor girl is smart in school, but we cannot seem to get her medicine regimen right. I gave her mother money for a blood transfusion, but recovery doesn't look promising, then I went back to the girl with failing grades.

A blind man with his little boy leading him came into the office next asking for school supplies. This man's wife died, and his other kids are grown and away. They live in extreme poverty. Next, was the uncle of one of our girls who used to live in the rescue home. He notified us that she was starting to have convulsions regularly. Months before he took her out of the home because he said he believed it was cursed. Now he wants our help again. We said we would meet with them next week when the office was not so busy.

There were at least 10 other issues we managed to handle yesterday.

Today has been a bit calmer. This morning started with me stripping my bed to change sheets and throwing them in the washing machine. That is a huge gift that really lightens my load. I now have had it for 4 years. I then made instant coffee, checked emails for possible hostel bookings, and had breakfast while reading my devotionals. My cat Kiki, who I picked up as a tiny kitten on the side of the road, sat with me. Kiki is more like a dog, the way she follows me everywhere on the property. Sometimes she wanders down to the hostel rooms. She often gets a guest to let her snuggle with them in bed at night.

After the washer was finished, I hung out the sheets and towels from the machine and headed over to the office, Kiki dutifully marching guard.

At the office, I opened more emails. I had to reply to two sponsors who want to know why their kids aren't "top of the class" in school. Sigh. I sometimes wish the sponsors could see where these kids come from. One is having trouble because the Primary 5 class is 100% in English, and she is from a child-headed family deep in a village. The other student is having trouble seeing, so I am sending her to get an eye exam.

I had to stop writing just now because 11 bikes were delivered that we are giving to students who must commute a long way to school. One is a small girl in secondary school who walks 11 kilometers each way every day. She leaves home at 5 am and returns at 7 pm yet still does well in class.

What do I do all day??? I can never say until the day comes.

Tomorrow, I have an appointment to work on writing a trust contract. I'm working out some serious legal details for the vocational center (no end while that's still birthing!).

Next week, an adoptive family, mother, dad, granddad and adopted 12-year-old, are coming back for a 9-day visit, and a church group from here is bringing 56 kids to the hostel for two days.

As I near the end of my story, I realize it's not an end at all. Any moment, 260 students from 40 different schools will start steaming in to eagerly (a few not so eagerly) come show me their first term school reports. So, dear readers, thank you for listening. I love what I do. I love where I am. Revisiting old challenges and joys has been a welcomed journey.

Final Word

Too often we are made to believe that we are supposed to accomplish certain milestones at a particular age, and we tend to feel like failures when we don't. We are told, finish school, get a good paying job, buy a house, settle down with a romantic partner, have children, contribute to the world and live happily ever after.

If this has been your experience, I'm happy for you.

But for most of us, life is not that straight forward. If we measure our sense of accomplishments against these society standards, we can set ourselves up for dissatisfaction and a never-ending cycle of self-criticism.

These arbitrary markers of success sometimes can make us miserable if we do not hit them.

Dear reader,

I would like to let you know that wherever you are today, at whatever age, you are still on a launching pad to start anew if you so choose.

If you are to successfully navigate life in a nonconventional way, you need to break free from society's powerful and often unrealistic expectations and embrace your own individual magic. Building this mindset takes time and involves dropping the guilt and re-adjusting your world view, but it's doable.

Instead of focusing on what society and others expect of you, you need to start a dialogue with yourself about what YOU truly want, and go do that.

I would like to let you know that your dreams and convictions of where you would like to take your life are valid. If acted upon, can change the world. You can start today. Crawl before you walk, walk before you run and before you know it, you will be flying.

I would like you to know that if your life is a full picture, today is just one pixel. Keep building that big picture one pixel at a time. Over the years, I have learned that playing the long game is the most direct way to have a positive impact in the world. One pixel at a time. Don't forget to honor and celebrate your accomplishments big or small along the way. Things like being a loving mom, father, sister, brother, a generous friend and a kindhearted coworker. Find a sense of meaning in bringing goodness in your immediate world even if it goes unnoticed. Too often we underestimate the power of a dollar, a touch, a smile, a kind word, a listening ear, or the smallest act of caring, all of which have the potential to turn a life around.

Though I started my social work later in life, I was able to live out my dreams. If I can do it, anyone can, and it's never too late. I am a living testament that all of us can affect change in our own capacities. We just have to manage our expectations and self judgement.

My sincere wish for you is that you embrace your

own unique superpowers. It's never too late to make a positive impact in the world.

Now, back to work.

Acknowledgements

I have so very many people to thank throughout my lifetime. I first want to thank Christopher Helms Ategeka whose encouragement convinced me to write this book as well as many others who kept saying, "You should write a book!" I also want to thank Rosalinda Sanquiche who worked tirelessly in helping to put together my many scattered and unorganized stories into a logical order.

Thank you, Lindsey Hampton for being supportive of my work all the way back from your peace corps service days here in Uganda and now for helping with editing the manuscript.

There are so very many others that it would take many pages to name them all. From my earlier years, I thank my late sister for being a mother to me. Later, the Olcott family made a huge difference by taking me in as if I were family.

In Hawaii, again, it would fill many pages to mention all of the wonderful people who made such a difference. Peter and Elizabeth Kaiama and family were the first to welcome me to Maui and teach me the ways of their Island. Other dear friends throughout the years there include church pastors Reverend Blomoerly and Reverend Tom from Po'okela Church in Makawao; Wendie and Steve Rhody and family; Dave and Ruth Fullaway and family; Patty and Loren Adams, and so many others who made such a difference in my life.

My early years in Uganda also gave me much needed people who were there for me. The very first would be Rose Musoke who took care of the "crazy mzungu" who was somewhat lost in Kampala. From there, Simeon Wiehlor rescued me and gave me a place at his home for boys in Mukono until I decided my next directions. From there, I ended up in Fort Portal and Reverend Charles Ndolerere was very welcoming. I also thank God for so many others who directed and taught me so much about Uganda. They include Norman and Isabel Jackson; Moses Magezi, now Dr. Magezi; Edwin and Ellen Bajenja; Reverend and Abwooli Rwakalembe; Mariam and Stephan Kluge; and again, so many others that I cannot name them all.

Lastly but certainly not least, thank you to the huge number of donors whose generosity has kept our program going these past 24 years: Waipuna Chapel, Maui HI; St. John's church, Oakland, CA; Rachel and Bertie Tracey of Ireland as well as Lucan Church and many individuals from a generous Ireland. From Germany, the Bender organization; Chancen fuer Kinder und Jugenliche; Carolyn Vom Stein, now Stauss and family; Willy and Waltraud Bonsels; Gudrun Bauer and other individual sponsors. From Canada, we have Arif

Alibhai with the HEAL organization. There are also hundreds of individual donors from all over the world who contribute either non-designated funds or money sent for specific children whose progress they follow through the school years.

Russell and Tara Karaviotis have played a huge part, helping me many times with my medical challenges by flying me to California and supporting me during those difficult times.

Again, I know I have left so many names out, but my heart is filled with gratitude towards God who has placed many people in my life just as I have needed them.

Made in United States
North Haven, CT
15 February 2023

32660419R00157